CAMBRIDGE LIBRARY COLLECTION

Books of enduring scholarly value

Cambridge

The city of Cambridge received its royal charter in 1201, having already been home to Britons, Romans and Anglo-Saxons for many centuries. Cambridge University was founded soon afterwards and celebrates its octocentenary in 2009. This series explores the history and influence of Cambridge as a centre of science, learning, and discovery, its contributions to national and global politics and culture, and its inevitable controversies and scandals.

Portrait of a College

This affectionate but far from sentimental history was published in 1961 to mark the 450th anniversary of the foundation of St John's College, Cambridge. Edward Miller (1915–2000) was a medieval historian who spent most of his career teaching in Cambridge. An undergraduate and research fellow at St John's, he later went on to become Master of Fitzwilliam. His 'Portrait' blends the history of St John's with wider developments in education, as well as social, political and economic history. As such it is a fine example of an institutional history written from within, with an unbiased assessment of the many changes the College had seen. The chapter on the period from 1918 to the early sixties, based on Miller's own reminiscences and those of his colleagues, is an important record of life in the college in an age of modernization and change.

T0381839

Cambridge University Press has long been a pioneer in the reissuing of out-of-print titles from its own backlist, producing digital reprints of books that are still sought after by scholars and students but could not be reprinted economically using traditional technology. The Cambridge Library Collection extends this activity to a wider range of books which are still of importance to researchers and professionals, either for the source material they contain, or as landmarks in the history of their academic discipline.

Drawing from the world-renowned collections in the Cambridge University Library, and guided by the advice of experts in each subject area, Cambridge University Press is using state-of-the-art scanning machines in its own Printing House to capture the content of each book selected for inclusion. The files are processed to give a consistently clear, crisp image, and the books finished to the high quality standard for which the Press is recognised around the world. The latest print-on-demand technology ensures that the books will remain available indefinitely, and that orders for single or multiple copies can quickly be supplied.

The Cambridge Library Collection will bring back to life books of enduring scholarly value across a wide range of disciplines in the humanities and social sciences and in science and technology.

Portrait of a College

A History of the College of Saint John the Evangelist in Cambridge

EDWARD MILLER

CAMBRIDGE UNIVERSITY PRESS

CAMBRIDGE UNIVERSITY PRESS

Cambridge New York Melbourne Madrid Cape Town Singapore São Paolo Delhi

Published in the United States of America by Cambridge University Press, New York

www.cambridge.org
Information on this title: www.cambridge.org/9781108003544

This edition first published 1961
This digitally printed version 2009

ISBN 978-1-108-00354-4

PORTRAIT OF
A COLLEGE

MARGARETA · MATER · HENRICI · SEPTIMI · ⬦ · COMITISSA · RICHMONDIE · ET · DARBIE · FUNDTRIX · COLLEGIORUM · CHRI · ET · IOANS · CANTABRIGIE · OBIIT · ANNO · DM̄ · 1 5 0 9 · KALEND · IVLII

THE LADY MARGARET BEAUFORT

PORTRAIT OF A COLLEGE

A HISTORY OF THE COLLEGE OF SAINT JOHN THE EVANGELIST CAMBRIDGE

BY

EDWARD MILLER

FELLOW AND COLLEGE LECTURER
IN HISTORY

CAMBRIDGE
AT THE UNIVERSITY PRESS
1961

PUBLISHED BY

THE SYNDICS OF THE CAMBRIDGE UNIVERSITY PRESS

Bentley House, 200 Euston Road, London, N.W.1
American Branch: 32 East 57th Street, New York 22, N.Y.
West African Office: P.O. Box 33, Ibadan, Nigeria

©

THE MASTER, FELLOWS AND SCHOLARS
OF ST JOHN'S COLLEGE CAMBRIDGE

1961

Printed in Great Britain at the University Press, Cambridge
(Brooke Crutchley, University Printer)

IN MEMORY OF

E. A. BENIANS

MASTER

AND

H. P. W. GATTY

FELLOW AND LIBRARIAN

OF

ST JOHN'S COLLEGE

CAMBRIDGE

CONTENTS

LIST OF ILLUSTRATIONS

PREFACE

A VENTURE into modern history on the part of a medievalist perhaps calls for a word of explanation. The imminence of the 450th anniversary of the college's foundation, falling in 1961, persuaded the council to invite me to survey once again the history of the college. After seeking to discharge that responsibility, I am more than ever convinced that the history of St John's is still to be written on the scale and in the detail the subject warrants. Time made it essential for me to concentrate upon a few main themes: upon the history of the college as a place of education and a community of human beings, and upon the relationship of the college to the changing society of the last four centuries. This is, therefore, a partial and pro-visional essay; and for that reason, for the convenience of those who wish to go deeper, I have added to it a short bibliography and notes indicating some of the main sources I have used. These I have placed at the end in order that they do not distract those who are willing to rest content with that part of the college's story I have sought to tell with a certain brevity.

Even in going so far as I have done, I have incurred many obligations. I must put first my indebtedness to members of the college staff: to Mr A. E. Martin, chief clerk; to Mr W. T. Thurbon and Mr R. B. Badcock in the bursary; to Mr N. Buck and his assistants in the college library; and to Miss B. Warboys, the senior tutor's secretary. All have shown a patience, as well as a knowledge, apparently illimitable. Mrs B. Chapman typed the bibliography and notes, thus greatly easing the task of the printer; and I must thank those who have permitted me to reproduce photographs, Mr J. W. Goodison for putting at my disposal his knowledge of the college portraits and Mr Edward Leigh for the skill with which he made the prints for the frontispiece and Plates I, IV, V and VI. Information and suggestions on particular matters were provided by Dr R. E. Robinson, Dr H. W. Howard and Dr N. F. M. Henry; and the Master (Mr J. S. Boys Smith), Mr F. P. White and Dr G. C. Evans read the text in draft and made many observations from which I greatly profited. To my wife I owe the title of

the book and gratitude for her forbearance when plans for the summer of
1960 were shipwrecked by the need to compose it. Mr Frank Thistle-
thwaite relieved me of most cares regarding publication and format; and
I have had the unstinted co-operation of Mr R. J. L. Kingsford, Mr Brooke
Crutchley, Mr R. A. Becher and the staff of the Cambridge University
Press. Finally, I have ventured to dedicate this essay to the memory of
two historians who taught me to see the history of the college as something which had a significance in English history and who, besides that,
showed me many personal kindnesses. I could have wished to convey
more adequately the things that I learned from them.

E. M.

ST JOHN'S COLLEGE, CAMBRIDGE

5 December 1960

I

BEGINNINGS
(1511-1537)

FOUR hundred and fifty years ago, on 9 April 1511, the executors of the
Lady Margaret Beaufort appended their seals to formal letters which
announced the birth of a new college in the University of Cambridge. In
Thomas Baker's summary, those letters set forth the 'desolate state' of the
old Hospital of St John, 'the intention of the foundress for dissolving [that]
house and annexing it to the college to be erected', and the various licences
obtained to this end. In virtue of these licences the executors 'did thereby
erect, ordain and establish a perpetual college' to consist of a master, fellows and scholars to the number of fifty or thereabouts *in scientiis liberalibus
et sacra theologia studentium et oraturorum*. It was to be called St John's College, to be a corporate body with a common seal and to be empowered to
purchase and receive lands for its upkeep. Robert Shorton was designated
first master and three nominees of the bishop of Ely were 'taken and elected
...to be fellows and scholars'. The executors retained power to nominate
further fellows and, 'if that number were not completed during their lives,
the master and fellows...might fill up that number'. Finally, the master's
authority to govern fellows and scholars was made plain, although in certain matters he was to be under an obligation to call together all the fellows
in order to obtain their consent to action he proposed.[1]

I

This charter is at once a beginning and an end. Its sequel will be the concern of this book; but, in order to discover the true original of the idea
which was realized in the college's foundation, we need to go back a few

years beyond 1511.[1] This journey takes us into the household of the Lady Margaret Beaufort, mother of King Henry VII and already a great benefactress to the university. She had established a professorship (originally called a readership) in divinity both at Cambridge and at Oxford; she had instituted 'a perpetual public preacher at Cambridge…to preach at least six sermons every year at several churches'; and in 1505, by the advice and persuasion of John Fisher, bishop of Rochester, she had enlarged the endowments and buildings of God's House, given it new statutes and modernized its name to Christ's College. Not unnaturally, at this point, she seems to have thought her work for Cambridge done and to have meditated a joint benefaction with her son to Westminster Abbey. John Fisher, however, had other thoughts. His eye had been caught by the thirteenth-century Hospital of St John in Cambridge, in some decay in its latter days, and his position as the Lady Margaret's chaplain gave weight to his suggestions for making better use of it. A plan to convert this hospital into a college was apparently discussed by the Lady Margaret's council as early as 1505, but it was not easy to bring her mind to this new enterprise. There was a period of indecision, and she caused Humphrey Conningsby, one of her counsellors, 'to make divers drafts at divers several times of her testament and last will…and most commonly about the feast of the Nativity of our Lord upon seven and eight years before her decease and more, caused her testament and will to be read unto her and renewed after her mind and pleasure'. For all this annual exercise Fisher's ideas for the St John's Hospital made slow progress. When the final version of the Lady Margaret's written testament was drawn up on 6 June 1508, the foundation of St John's College was still not mentioned in it.

As the Lady Margaret's life drew to a close, however, Fisher was getting his way. After she was dead, those who had been about her were able to bear testimony that she 'made and declared her said will often and many times by her mouth' to translate St John's Hospital into a college of which she would be 'chief foundress and patroness'. She did more than give verbal expression to this intention. Sometime in 1508 she summoned to her house at Hatfield the bishop of Ely, whose diocesan authority extended over the hospital. They discussed the suppression and conversion of the hospital and drew up a formal agreement to achieve this end on 10 March 1509. The bishop, however, seems never to have signed it, for mortality came to play its part. Henry VII (who had likewise agreed to abandon their joint plans for a benefaction to Westminster) died on 21 April 1509 and his mother on 29 June following. At this juncture the Lady Margaret's intention to translate hospital into college was still only a matter of words.

In those days, however, before writing was a common accomplishment, a verbal will was fully valid provided it could be duly proven. Everything depended, therefore, upon the Lady Margaret's executors and, chief among them, John Fisher. More was at stake than the transfer of St John's Hospital to provide the site and initial endowment for the college. That arrangement needed confirmation, but would by itself have been sparse provision for the new foundation. On the other hand, the Lady Margaret had assigned the revenues from certain of her lands in Devon, Somerset and Northamptonshire, worth in all some £400 yearly, to fulfil her last will and testament. Proof that it had been her intention to dissolve the hospital and annex it to the college to be erected would enable these funds to be used to provide the new foundation with buildings, to furnish it with books and ornaments and to purchase real property for its endowment.

That the Lady Margaret's words were translated into deeds was, in the main, the achievement of John Fisher. On 7 August 1509 he won the backing of the new king, Henry VIII, and he went on to secure papal licence for the suppression of the hospital through the intermediacy of Polydore Vergil. With this authority behind him he won the concurrence of the bishop of Ely on 12 December 1510, on consideration that the latter's jurisdiction over the new college was accepted and that the present bishop might nominate three, and his successors one, of the fellows. Very soon the bishop's chancellor was 'tarrying in Cambridge...to induce the late brethren of St John's to resign'; on 20 January 1511 the executors of the Lady Margaret were given possession of the hospital; and on 12 March its remaining brethren 'departed from Cambridge towards Ely...at four of the clock at afternoon by water'. The way was clear for the letters of foundation and the installation of Robert Shorton as first master in April.

Difficulties were not over at this point. The new collegiate community did not yet exist. In order that it might exist, new funds and new buildings were required; for the hospital revenues amounted only to £50 yearly and its premises were inadequate and in ill-repair. Thus, to establish the college it was necessary to have a call for some time upon income from the estates which the Lady Margaret had assigned for the fulfilment of her last will and testament. An initial obstacle was the fact that the plan to found the college found no place in the Lady Margaret's written will. Fisher's first task was to prove in the court of the archbishop of Canterbury that this had indeed been her intention, a task successfully completed when a codicil to this effect was appended to her written testament on 22 October 1512. With this warrant the court of Chancery in November empowered her executors to receive the issues of her estates to build and endow the college. There was still another problem: sooner or later the question was bound to arise as to when the Lady Margaret's intentions had been sufficiently realized for her estates, from which the college was drawing revenue, to revert to her heir-at-law, Henry VIII. In the event the question arose sooner rather than later, for the king's financial officers had a natural concern for his interests. The outcome was, as Fisher said, that 'we were more straitly handled and so long delayed and wearied and fatigate that we must needs let the lands go'.

Disappointment at what seemed the premature curtailment of the Lady Margaret's benefaction gave birth to a hardy legend that she had intended her lands, not for the temporary provision of capital to establish the college, but for its permanent endowment. This legend has its basis in that passage of Fisher's statutes of 1524, in which he states that it had proved impossible to found the full complement of fifty fellowships which the Lady Margaret had intended, *ob subtractionem reddituum annuorum ad valorem quadringentarum librarum.* The passage need imply no more than that these revenues were withdrawn *too early;* but, after it had been reproduced in the statutes of 1530 and 1545, it was turned easily into an article of faith that the Lady

4

Margaret had meant her benefaction to be a perpetual gift. This point of view was put to Queen Elizabeth I when she visited Cambridge in 1564. She 'rode into the hall, where she was received with an oration by Mr Bohun; wherein she was put in mind of her relation to the foundress and intimation given of the college losses'. It was with good ground in law, however, that 'the queen did not think herself bound to take notice of those losses'.[1]

Henry VIII, on the other hand, may not have been quite without a sense that he had acted precipitately. Apparently he promised the college £2800 due to him for a wardship and, when this produced in fact only £1200, co-operated in 1516 in securing the dissolution of the Maison Dieu at Ospringe (Kent) and the transfer of its property to the college. Fisher also had the king's support in securing for it in 1526 the possessions of two other decayed religious houses—the nunneries of Lilliechurch in Kent and Broomhall in Berkshire. In addition, Fisher expended money and treasure belonging to the Lady Margaret, in his hands as her executor, upon additional endowments; and he established and endowed four fellowships and two scholarships from his own resources. In the meantime, too, 'private founders were crowding in'.[2] Some, like Hugh Ashton (whose altar-tomb still stands in the college chapel), were men of the Lady Margaret's circle; and others, including Henry Ediall, archdeacon of Rochester, were closely associated with Fisher. Some were clergymen, like John Dowman, who endowed five scholarships for Pocklington boys and nine sizarships, or Roger Lupton, founder of two fellowships and eight scholarships attached to Sedbergh school. Others again were layfolk, like Sir Marmaduke Constable or Sir Richard Rokeby's widow.

Their benefactions took various forms. Fisher himself gave a good deal of land, including property in the Holbeach district which remains the nucleus of the college's Lincolnshire estate; and Sir Marmaduke Constable provided in like manner for his scholars by the gift of his Yorkshire manor at Millington. Hugh Ashton and Roger Lupton, on the other hand, gave money; while Thomas Thimbleby's and Dr Fell's bequests took the form of money, plate and jewels. The end result, however, was always the same.

Benefactions in money or treasure were invested in land in order to provide a continuing revenue to fulfil the purposes which donors had envisaged. In this way the college quickly came to be a landowning corporation which depended primarily upon rents to meet its outgoings. The original nucleus of hospital property in Cambridgeshire and the adjoining counties was augmented by the Lady Margaret's manor at Fordham (Cambs), which the college was probably enabled to purchase because the foundress's will had allotted it to extinguish her debts; by the Kentish properties of Ospringe and Lilliechurch, of which a good deal is still in the college's hands; and by the Broomhall properties in Surrey, Berkshire and Oxfordshire, including much of what is now the college's Sunningdale estate. It was increased still further by private benefactions and the investment of benefactions, which took the landowning interests of the college still further afield. Despite all the difficulties, Fisher's pertinacity and the generosity of benefactors provided the college with a revenue which may well have exceeded the best hopes of the earliest days. Already £224 in 1518, it had risen to £500 in 1534—a considerable sum in the time before the great inflation of the century which followed.

All this has taken us far from the college's first beginnings: but the provision of money was a condition for bringing it into existence, and for this reason it was fortunate that Robert Shorton 'was a man of business as well as learning'. He was the financial manager on the spot and it was his achievement that 'under his care and conduct...the building rose'. His responsibility for this work began before he became master, for he took charge on 31 January 1511 and, before he closed his accounts early in 1516, he had spent £4772 on the fabric of the college ('a round sum in that age').[1] The results of his labours can still be seen in first court, which encompassed the whole of the college as Shorton built it. Bricks were supplied by Richard Reculver of Greenwich, Oliver Scales was clerk of works and Richard Wright of Bury St Edmund's contractor for the hall and chapel windows. Most of the present eastern range of the court survives, including the gate tower decorated with Tudor heraldry and accommodating treasury and porters' lodge, and on the first floor to the south of the gate the original library, easily recognized by its distinctive windows. The western range, too, is much as Shorton built it and it contained then, as now, the kitchens, buttery and hall (though the last was considerably shorter than it is today). The north and south ranges, on the other hand, have been more drastically changed since the sixteenth century. The latter was heightened and faced with stone by James Essex in 1772 and the former was destroyed to make way for the new chapel in the nineteenth century. The founders of the college took over and refurbished the thirteenth-century chapel of the hospital and extended it to join up with the hall range, providing accommodation in the process for a combination room and master's lodging. Of this all that remains is the chapel outline marked out in stone on the lawns beside the newer chapel. The hospital infirmary, which lay behind the chapel and which was likewise demolished in the nineteenth century, was also retained to serve at first as a stable and storehouse. For the rest, in the beginning, between the single court and the river were gardens and trees and some remains of the hospital buildings; and beyond the river, across a wooden bridge, lay fishponds to the north and a meadow to the south, separated by a ditch which joined the Bin brook to the Cam.[1]

First court, then, catered for all the needs of the original community. It contained the domestic offices and library already mentioned; the chapel for divine service and a variety of other college occasions; the hall where much college instruction was dispensed as well as meals; and living quarters for fellows and scholars. Accommodation was anything but lavish. The master allotted rooms or chambers, and only doctors of divinity and college preachers might have rooms to themselves. Other chambers were to contain two beds, a 'higher' bed for a fellow and a truckle bed for one or two students (although, unless the latter were under fourteen years of age, not more than two of them were to share a bed). Propinquity was not merely a matter of making accommodation go round: it also had disciplinary and educational objects. Fisher ordained that 'the older should advise their younger chamber-mates, give them good encouragement and show them good example, instruct them in discipline, draw their attention to...repeated trespasses and misdoing and, if necessary, report them...to the

7

master, president or deans'. Modern generations might find this a life confined in more ways than one.[1]

The building of the college, not quite completed until 1520, was in a fair way to being finished in 1516, enabling it to be opened on or about 29 July. The occasion coincided with Shorton's resignation of the mastership and the succession of Alan Percy, the latter being succeeded in turn by Nicholas Metcalfe, Fisher's chaplain and archdeacon of Rochester, in 1518. If Shorton is remembered as the builder of the college, Metcalfe was the establisher of its corporate life. Fuller summed up his achievement in his own inimitable way: 'Metcalfe with Themistocles could not fiddle, yet he knew how to make a little college a great one.'[2] There were beginnings, it is true, under his predecessors, for we find Shorton writing to Fisher about potential fellows who were thought to be 'good, virtuous and learned and men tractable';[3] but Baker is undoubtedly correct when he says 'we are not to imagine...that there was any settled society or school of learning under this period,...only four or five fellows maintained by the college (and no scholars)...and these were lodged abroad...so that they kept no exercise or discipline in the college'. Numbers soon grew, however, after it was opened, reaching thirty-five in 1518 and fifty-two in 1519. Eventually the basic establishment came to be the master with twenty-eight fellows and twenty-two scholars of the Lady Margaret's foundation; and to this initial complement private founders added by 1545 sixteen fellows and thirty-six scholars, and the total number in residence had risen to 152. This was rapid growth indeed in less than thirty years, and in 1528 Metcalfe had to begin building additional accommodation occupying a site in the south-east corner of the later second court. It was demolished when that court was built.[4]

II

The community which Shorton and Metcalfe assembled required rules to guide it and again it was John Fisher who provided them. He drew up three sets of statutes (in 1516, 1524 and 1530), which afford a picture of the college's formal constitution and glimpses of the educational practice which was designed to achieve its proper ends.[5] They vested the government of the college in a master elected by the fellows. There was also a president to act as his deputy, while in important matters the master was to act according to the advice and with the consent of the seven senior fellows. Two bursars were responsible in financial matters and two deans for discipline, and a steward was appointed monthly from the ranks of the fellows to supervise the provision of meals in hall. These officers were assisted by a staff which is exiguous by later standards: a maniple working under the steward, two cooks, a servant for the master, a porter, a barber, and a laundress who (in the interests of propriety) was to penetrate no further into the college than the gate.

The main elements of the community were the scholars and the fellows. Scholars were chosen by the master, seniors and officers after examination in singing and letters; and, other things being equal, the poorer candidates had preference over the less poor. Place of birth, however, was also important. The Lady Margaret's intention had been that at least half her scholars should come from the nine northern counties and, of those from the southern counties, men born in six of them had advantage over the rest. Scholarships of private foundation, too, were subject to divers limitations. John Dowman's and Roger Lupton's were restricted to boys from particular schools; others gave preference to the kin of the founder or to candidates from a particular district, often narrowly defined. Hugh Ashton's scholars, for example, had to come from Lancashire, Yorkshire and Durham or from the dioceses of Chester, York and Durham; while first claim to the Thimbleby scholarship was given to one of Dr Thimbleby's name and kin and, after that, there was some preference for sons of tenants upon Dr Thimbleby's property.[1] The award of foundress's and privately endowed fellowships was governed by precisely similar rules and the picture was further complicated by the regulation that, save in exceptional circumstances, there should not be at any one time more than two scholars and two fellows born in any one county. Fisher appears to envisage the relaxation of this last rule should it prove possible to increase the number of foundress's fellows. In fact that never was possible, and what probably originated as a device to spread scarce fellowships and scholarships among

9

candidates from many different parts of England (though with a preference for northerners) came to be an inconvenience of great longevity.
Thus, for fellows as for scholars, some luck as to place of birth was required
from the beginning: that apart, a fellow had to be a graduate, preferably
a priest and normally a man intending to study theology. He was chosen
by the master and all fellows in residence from a list of candidates for which
any fellow might suggest names.

Master, fellows and scholars constituted the whole body of the college
in Fisher's original statutes of 1516, but his later codes add a new element.
Pensioners supported by their families or friends might also be admitted,
provided that their qualifications were approved by the master and seniors
and that they promised to perform all scholastic exercises and attend divine
service. They might include, moreover, eight noblemen and fellow commoners (that is, undergraduates who ate at the somewhat more generously
provided fellows' table)—but again with the admonition *dummodo sub
tutela et regimine extiterint*. The decision to introduce noblemen, fellow
commoners and pensioners was of major importance. In the long run, it
helped substantially to alter the part the college played in English life, to
diversify its composition, to impose new demands upon its educational
provision and to modify the purposes which the Lady Margaret and John
Fisher had designed it to serve.

The purposes of the college, as the foundress and her executor envisaged
them, are succinctly summarized in a single phrase of the statutes: *Dei cultus,
morum probitas et Christianae fidei corroboratio*. They thought of it, in other
words, as something more than an educational institution, at least in our
limited sense. It was to be a community living the religious life, in which
the round of chapel services would not be ranked inferior to scholastic
exercises; in which seniors would instruct juniors by precept and example,
not only in things of the mind, but in conduct and probity of life; and
in which the day would begin and end with private prayer and include a
daily mass, the remembrance of benefactors in prayers, and bible reading
in hall. The links between this collegiate and the older monastic ways of
living are obvious enough. They are also suggested by the rules restraining

undergraduates from leaving the college save for lectures and instruction, even if these rules failed to prevent William Cecil finding his way to Mrs Cheke's wine shop, attracted by John Cheke's sister, Mary, who was soon to be his wife.[1] A similar inference is to be drawn from the restrictions placed even upon graduates wishing to go out into the town; from the obligation placed upon fellows, scholars and even servants to have the tonsure; and from the incompatibility of a fellowship with the married state. John Fisher's notion of a college was, in many important respects, a very medieval thing.

So, too, in many ways, was his notion of the ultimate purpose which a college ought to serve. The foundress's design, he tells us, had been to establish a school of theology. The study of sacred theology, therefore, was envisaged in his statutes as the goal of all studies and normally all fellows had to assume priest's orders within a specified period. From this last rule he exempted only those fellows skilled in the medical art, an exemption restricted to two fellows only by the Elizabethan statutes of 1580. Here, however, is indication that Fisher did not see the college quite exclusively as a school of theology; and it is no less clear that he lacked any desire to make even the general body of the fellows into cloisterers. On the contrary, those whose study lay in the field of sacred theology, like those who studied the medical art, were to be trained for the service of society. The foundress's desire, we are told, had been that the fruits of her school of theology should be communicated to others. To this end, a quarter of the fellows were to be engaged in preaching to the people in English and there is an underlying assumption that all would sooner or later depart into the full-time active priesthood. A fellow had to resign if other commitments involved him in absence from the college for more than a month in the year, or if he had a benefice not tenable in plurality, or one worth more than £5 a year. Moreover, since a fellow's perquisites were relatively modest (a stipend of 13s. 4d. and 52s. for commons and livery), benefices offering more of this world's goods had some attraction. All in all, the college in its beginnings was not only in the main a school of theology: it was a school of practical theology.

Its curriculum was designed to this end, but not without indication of the presence of new wine in old bottles. Erasmus spoke in 1516, the year in which the college was opened, of the influx into Cambridge of the 'polite learning' of the Renaissance—mathematics, a 'regenerated Aristotle' and Greek studies. Fisher played an important part in encouraging this work of intellectual renovation and his interests leave a mark upon the academic system he provided for St John's.[1] Freshmen apparently began with mathematics, and four college lecturers in the subject were to be appointed for their instruction. Before the end of the first year, however, they proceeded to logic and philosophy, and a head lecturer and two sublecturers guided their steps through the Aristotelian system and the academic disputations which were the main method of testing intellectual capacity. At the same time, the college was also to have a Greek lecturer to teach grammar and literature daily; a Greek dictionary was one of the books bought for Fisher's scholars in 1530;[2] and, when Roger Ascham came up in that year, St John's was already a home of Greek learning, with Robert Pember, John Redman and above all John Cheke as its notable teachers. Ascham in his turn taught Greek to undergraduates younger than himself, and he gathered up a distinguished band of pupils after he became a fellow in 1534 and Greek lecturer in 1538.[3]

If only because it was so much a home of the new learning, the college (rather than the university) was called upon from the first to provide much of the teaching required by its undergraduates. The statutes envisaged that men might go to 'public' (that is, university) lectures, but they also made provision for circumstances in which public lectures would not be available or would be unsuitable for Johnians. For these reasons Fisher equipped it with a staff of college lecturers, who would supplement university provision, and also ordained that four 'examiners' should be appointed to give additional instruction when necessary and to 'question' pupils daily on the substance of college and university lectures. Thus, the prominence of 'polite learning' at St John's made it from the beginning a leader in the movement which was transferring responsibility for teaching from the medieval university to the more modern colleges. The single exception to this tendency in the college is perhaps to be discerned in the lectureship founded by Thomas Linacre, physician to Henry VIII, in 1534. The Linacre lecturer was, indeed, to observe the principles of lecturing prevalent in St John's rather than those of the university schools; he was to be well read in Aristotle and Galen; he was preferably to be a fellow of the college; but his lectures were to be in the public schools and open to all. His somewhat exceptional position among college lecturers is perhaps the counterpart of the exceptional position Fisher had allotted to fellows who were physicians.

When undergraduates had been taught, however, and proceeded after ten terms to the B.A. degree, the college's educational task was only half completed. It was assumed that most would stay for nine more terms in order to proceed M.A. and that some would continue as fellows longer still. Bachelors went on with the study of philosophy and, before their M.A. degree, had to expound publicly two books of Aristotle's *De Anima*. Fellows were expected to engage in three disputations weekly, twice in theology and once in philosophy with Duns Scotus as their guide; to study Hebrew under a college lecturer in that subject; and eventually, after showing their capacity by expounding twenty chapters of the New Testament, to proceed to the degree of bachelor in theology. The new learning might diversify the way, but the ultimate goal of an academic career was still that which the Lady Margaret had intended.

This long-drawn course of study (made longer by the fact that, since communications were difficult, residence and some instruction in vacations was normal) almost presupposed a very early age of entry. Fisher's statutes assume it to be possible for a scholar to be elected before he was fourteen; both William Cecil and Roger Ascham came up ,at fifteen; and the latter was a B.A. and a fellow by the time he was nineteen. The youthfulness of undergraduates and fellows makes more comprehensible some of the restrictions to which they were subjected, and even the fact that *pueri*, at least, might be whipped for tardiness or negligence at college lectures and exercises. There were, however, carefree interludes in college life. Undergraduates might play in the fields behind the college provided they went there in groups of not less than three. Archery was blessed as a recreation (though not within the precincts of the college), and Ascham was not only skilled in this sport but wrote a book about it. Again, when a fire was made up in the hall in a brazier beneath the lantern which still marks its position, fellows, scholars and servants might stay to amuse themselves with singing and repeating poetry and tales. The atmosphere is perhaps somewhat that of a modern boarding school, but that would accord well enough with the ages of most of the college community.

In this manner, then, did John Fisher execute the last will and testament of the Lady Margaret Beaufort. He presided over the erection of the college's fabric, its endowment as a landed corporation, the assembling of a body of fellows and scholars, the infusion into its undergraduate membership of pensioners and fellow commoners, and the settlement of its government and system of education. While he never betrayed the foundress's intention that the college should be a school of theology, the fruits of which would be communicated to others, he also made it the leading centre of Renaissance learning in Cambridge and even into a place in which students of the art of medicine might find a home. All this was the work of a mere quarter-century and there is justice in Baker's verdict (when all due tribute has been paid to the foundress's beneficence) that Fisher was 'the greatest patron the college ever had to this day'. But his religion was the old religion and this took him to the scaffold in 1535. Even at the end, however, the college did not forget its debt to him. It sent deputations to attend upon him in his imprisonment and wrote him a 'noble letter', from which one sentence deserves quotation for its intrinsic verity. *Tu nobis pater, doctor, praeceptor, legislator, omnis denique virtutis et sanctitatis exemplar. Tibi victum, tibi doctrinam, tibi quicquid est boni vel habemus vel scimus nos debere fatemur.*[1]

The winds of change which brought Fisher to the block did not blow only in high places: they also penetrated within the walls of the college. Most Johnians at first were opponents of the new ideas in religion, but Thomas Arthur was a member of Protestant circles as early as 1527 and was put on trial with Bilney.[2] The new ideas gained ground and Roger Ascham was one who was won over to them. Though Metcalfe championed him,[3]

14

I. JOHN FISHER, BISHOP OF ROCHESTER

the master was, after all, Fisher's protégé, loyal to Fisher's religious views and, perhaps, of old-fashioned academic opinions in some men's eyes. His position, in consequence, became increasingly uncomfortable within the college, faced with a new set of fellows inclined to Protestantism and 'addicted to a new and politer sort of learning'. He was also unpopular at court, and intimations from that quarter combined with the discontents of the 'young fry of fellows of St John's' to jostle him into retirement in 1537.[1] This episode reveals tendencies already at work which were to dominate the history of the college in the following age: the emergence of a new and more secular conception of learning, stemming from seeds which Fisher himself had helped to sow; the fragmentation of the undivided faith which was all the Lady Margaret had known and for which Fisher had died; the appearance of the monarchy as the decisive authority over colleges, university, church and nation alike. Not surprisingly, therefore, Metcalfe's resignation marked the beginning of a century and more of controversy and change. Yet he had built well enough, as Fisher's chief aide in the period of origins, to enable the college to weather the stresses of the ensuing generations. Roger Ascham was one of the 'young fry of fellows' in 1537—only twenty-two years old, addicted to Protestantism and a light of the new learning; but he did not forget in the new days his own and the college's debt to the old master. He spoke of him in later years with affection and tells us that Metcalfe 'left such a company of fellows and scholars at St John's College as can scarce be found now in some whole university'.[2] That is no unworthy memorial.

II

THE AGE OF CONTROVERSY
(1537-1661)

THE influences which lay behind Metcalfe's retirement very soon emerged into the foreground. For well over a century thereafter colleges were the centres of bitter religious controversies; it can be said, indeed, that 'early Puritanism, like early Protestantism, was an academic movement centred on the University of Cambridge'[1] and not least upon St John's College in that university. This followed inevitably from the fact that religious questions were the dominant intellectual issues of the day and from the very purposes served by academic studies. Those purposes were, as Roger Ascham defined them in 1547: 'first, that we may diffuse the Lord's gospel among God's people; then, that we may root out, in so far as we can, papism with all hypocrisy, superstition and idolatry'.[2] The circumstances of the Reformation gave to colleges a controversial role, and that role generated divisions within them which were often so deep as to be unbridgeable.

At the same time, such divisions could not be purely private matters. They also concerned the rulers of England because colleges were 'nurseries of ideas and opinions' and trained others besides candidates for the priesthood. Ascham again has pointed to the dual role they were coming to play: *in vineam Domini mittimus plurimos operarios; in reliquam rempublicam aptos et instructos viros.*[3] The climate of opinion in colleges, therefore, was of general and not merely of ecclesiastical significance. Further, the Reformation resulted in the subjection of the colleges and the university, in a manner unique among ecclesiastical institutions, to the royal supremacy. They were exempted even from the metropolitan jurisdiction of the archbishop of Canterbury and therefore peculiarly exposed to the authority of the Crown. Government interference in their internal affairs, in consequence, became frequent and far-reaching. The effects were, perhaps, felt particularly in St John's. It was a notable centre of Puritan tendencies at a time when religion bred men firm for principle who did not always count the cost of being so. It was also the college of William Cecil, Lord Burghley. He had a real affection for his 'old nurse', which made him watchful of what he took to be its interests; and he became Queen Elizabeth's first minister and chancellor of Cambridge University. He had not only a personal concern for the college's welfare, but official power to intervene authoritatively in its affairs.

I

The royal supremacy made itself felt, however, long before Cecil attained a position of power. Fisher was hardly dead when Thomas Cromwell ordered his fishes on the choir stalls to be transformed into 'monstrous and ugly antics'. His tomb, too, in the chantry he had built for his burial and remembrance between the chapel and the old infirmary, was defaced;[1] and all that remains today of Fisher's projected memorial are the arches built into the south wall of the modern ante-chapel. No less significant, however, was the making of a master to succeed Metcalfe. Cromwell granted the college's request for a free election, but at the same time drew its attention to Dr George Day, much in favour at court as the author of the university's decree on the royal supremacy. The fellows were not persuaded and chose Fisher's and Metcalfe's friend, Nicholas Wilson, but he judged it wiser to refuse; so Day in the end was elected, only to resign in a year. In his place John Taylor, a Lutheran and one of the compilers of the Book of Common Prayer, was brought to be master by the king's command from Queens' College. It would seem that too many fellows were still too set in old ways for a free election.

Protestantism was growing, however, and under Taylor's rule internal dissensions came into the open. Some fellows suffered expulsion; disputes between fellows, and between the fellows and the master, called for intervention by the bishop of Ely as visitor; and Roger Ascham was so perturbed in 1544 that his father was advising him to seek his living elsewhere.[1] These circumstances occasioned another manifestation of the royal supremacy: Henry VIII gave new statutes to the college in 1545. They expunged all mention of Fisher and added his scholarships and fellowships to those established by the foundress. They also made two sets of changes particularly relevant to the current situation: the powers of the master were considerably augmented; and the number of northern fellows (perhaps the nucleus of the traditionalist party) was to be in future *not more* than (instead of *at least*) half the total body, with a like proportion prevailing among the seniors.[2] These statutes, however, seem merely to have provoked 'new heats' and Taylor was eventually driven to resign in 1547. He was succeeded by William Bill, friend of John Cheke (a former fellow and Edward VI's tutor), brother of the court physician and a protégé of Protector Somerset. Heartily in favour of the Reformation himself, he was still not so warm as others and it was a group led by Thomas Lever which made the pace. Bill, in fact, perhaps accepted translation to Trinity with relief in 1551, leaving the way open for Lever to succeed him. The latter was already known as a great and fearless preacher (as Baker says, his sermons 'would have spoiled any man's preferment at this day') and under him 'the Reformation nowhere gained more ground or was more zealously maintained than it did here under this master's example and the influence of his government'.[3]

For this reason the college was particularly affected by the Marian reaction. In 1553 Lever himself and fourteen fellows went into exile, provoking Ascham to observe that 'more perfect scholars were dispersed from there in a month than many years can rear up again'.[4] With the accession of Elizabeth I, however, some of them returned from the centres of continental Protestantism; and two, the brothers James and Leonard Pilkington, were masters from 1559 to 1564, continuing and developing Lever's work in the spirit of Calvin. During their time Thomas Cartwright and William Fulke were fellows and 'infected the college with an almost incurable disaffection'; 'Popish trash' was removed from the chapel and

Geneva psalters were brought in; and part of Fisher's chantry chapel was turned into a room for the master.[1] There were perhaps grounds for the feeling in high places that St John's was falling into disorder.

It was true, at least, that Calvinist enthusiasm was dividing the fellowship into two hostile camps. Trouble came to a head under Leonard Pilkington's successor, Richard Longworth, although William Fulke rather than Longworth turned dissension into crisis. Fulke's sermons persuaded the college to sell its copes and many fellows and undergraduates to appear in chapel on 13 October 1565 without their surplices. Longworth was out of Cambridge at the time, but he condoned the incident which made internecine battle in St John's a national affair. The vice-chancellor and Cecil were brought into it, and the latter found an instrument in Richard Curteys, the president of the college. Cecil committed its government to Curteys for a time and Fulke was driven to lecture at the Falcon inn in Petty Cury. Longworth eventually scrambled out of his predicament and recovered his authority; but civil war in the college continued, by now as much a matter of 'private grudge and displeasure' as of anything else. Fulke, too, was allowed to return and, by a strange shift, was soon at odds with the master. In the end the latter was removed by the visitor and Fulke, his fire perhaps tempered by age, became ultimately a not undistinguished master of Pembroke College.[2]

For a time, after Longworth's removal, the college's quarrels lost their dramatic character. We may conjecture, with Cole, that his successor, Nicholas Shepherd, was brought in to tame the Puritan faction: for in his time the use of Geneva psalters in chapel was discontinued. It may be, however, that he did not go fast enough. He, too, was removed in 1574 and one ground alleged against him was 'encouragement of the precise party'. John Still (1574–7) was more determined to root out Puritanism, and in consequence stimulated opposition which made it impossible to hold fellowship elections during his last two years of office. When Still was removed to Trinity, therefore, Burghley took the situation firmly in hand. He seems to have been mainly responsible for securing the translation of Richard Howland from Magdalene to rule St John's and for the provision in 1580 of new statutes which governed the college down to the nine-teenth century. Significantly, they once again added to the powers of the master, a necessary step to tame an unruly body of fellows and one not to be feared because in practice the master was nominated by the Crown. Significantly, too, they took away from the powers of the visitor. In that connection we have to remember that royal powers of visitation were being constantly exercised in Cambridge and might be deemed more effective than those of the bishop of Ely to impose discipline on St John's. The import of the royal supremacy, in fact, was being brought home; and it was no more than politic for the college to assure Burghley in 1584 that Howland had established peace within it and promoted learning.[1]

New statutes, however, could not at once cause the 'factious party' to disappear or solve all problems, and Burghley's own principles might even create some of them. He was all for discipline and was determined that the college should not be a nurse of 'rash young heads that are so soon ripe to climb into pulpits' and that 'will content themselves with no limits in the church or in the polity'. On the other hand, his sympathies (like those of Archbishop Whitgift) were emphatically Protestant, and he saw no reason why discipline should not be achieved without theological backsliding. At the same time, things were altering in Cambridge.[2] The Calvinist doc-trines, which had secured a large following, were coming under fire; and in St John's opportunity was given for factions to revive by the fact that Howland, for two years before his resignation in 1587, had held his master-ship in plurality with the bishopric of Peterborough. Burghley again nominated his successor, though he may not have counted the consequences. William Whitaker was a scholar of distinction, but he was a determined defender of the Calvinist position and perhaps too deeply engaged by scholarship to keep his hands on all the reins of power. These fell, by his default and favour, to Henry Alvey, leader of the Puritan group among the fellows. Naturally this raised an opposition faction among those who envied Alvey's authority or detested his theology. There were rumours of 'synods' and 'presbyteries' in the college and the master came under fire for his Calvinism and his support of Alvey. He was accused of tyranny for expelling Everard Digby from his fellowship (though Digby's irresponsibility, if not his alleged Popish sympathies, were perhaps sufficient justification for this extreme step) and for making Alvey president in 1591, apparently against the wishes of a majority of the seniors. In brief, the old discords broke out again, producing a flow of complaints and appeals and petitions until the master died in December 1595.[1]

Whitaker was the last and perhaps the greatest of the ultra-Protestant masters, and his death was the end of an epoch. At once the anti-Puritan faction, conscious that it was slightly in a minority and fearing Alvey's succession, enlisted the aid of Burghley. The latter had now learned the danger represented by a Calvinist master and presented the fellows with a choice between two candidates who had belonged to the opposition in Whitaker's time. They chose Richard Clayton, who ruled the college until 1612—longer than any of his predecessors except Metcalfe.[2] Whether or not the problems of aesthetic taste involved in the building of second court offered 'a harmless but comparatively effective outlet for academic passions', factions subsided under Clayton and an Anglican reaction made rapid progress. 'Puritanism', as Baker says, 'was now in great measure rooted out',[3] to such an extent that, in 1612, it was considered safe to allow the fellows themselves to elect a master. Symptomatically, they chose Owen Gwyn, another of Alvey's enemies. He had some gifts as an administrator, but the court had nothing to fear from him. The college took a leading part in entertaining Prince Charles in 1612 and the king himself in 1613 (when Ben Jonson was asked to 'pen a ditty' for the royal delectation). It bore with equanimity the king's dispensing power, which thrust a Scot into a Cumberland fellowship and allowed a fellow to receive his emoluments when serving as a chaplain in the navy. Gwyn, too, pressed the claims of the courtier duke of Buckingham for the chancellorship of the university.[4] Royalism was joining hands with Anglicanism in St John's.

Unanimity of sentiment, however, did not prevent division. When Gwyn died in 1634 the succession to the mastership was disputed, and once again the royal supremacy was invoked. Charles I 'pitched upon a third man and sent his letters mandatory for Dr Beale' of Jesus College.[5] It may be unfair to call him (as Prynne did) 'a creature of Laud'; but, after Cosin of Peterhouse, he was certainly the most Laudian head of a house in Cambridge. His influence was soon seen in the college chapel. Within a year of his accession a London organ-maker, Robert Dallam, had built a 'pair of organs' for £185. This was not the first instrument the college had possessed, for there is record of a purchase of a 'pair of organs' as early as c. 1521; but nothing more is heard of them after 1557 and it may well be that Beale was seeking to remedy a total lack. In addition, he expected the fellows to contribute to the organist's salary and he probably inherited some sort of choir (in Gwyn's time a patron had recommended a poor boy to the master with the desire that 'you would vouchsafe to bestow on him a chorister's place in your chapel' or else a scholarship or sizarship). Beale also refurbished and redecorated the chapel and, according to Simonds D'Ewes, the well-known Puritan diarist who came up to St John's as a fellow commoner in 1618, 'caused such general adoration to and towards the altar and sacraments...that many godly fellows and scholars...left their places to avoid the abomination'.[1]

It is not, therefore, surprising that there were complaints of 'papistical innovations' or that Beale's policy in religion had political overtones. Robert Waideson, who became a fellow (ironically enough by royal mandate) in 1639, said later that the college 'was so fermented with the old traditions...that I could not digest their sour belches against the parliament'.[2] Beale himself was accused of preaching against the subject's freedom and he helped to compile Laud's canons of 1640, which demanded adherence on the part of members of the university to the doctrines of divine right and non-resistance. Thus it was natural enough that the college should entertain Charles I in 1642, when John Cleveland, fellow and cavalier poet, 'harangued' him; and that it smuggled the college plate out to him in the same year, including the tankard presented by Thomas Fairfax as well as the pot with two ears which had been the gift of Strafford. The day of reckoning soon came. Beale was arrested in September and despatched to London. In 1643 Cromwell was in command in Cambridge and the first court of the college served as a prison for two hundred delinquents; Beale's new organ and the pictures were removed from the chapel and its walls were made plain white; and the year ended with a visit from William Dowsing, who prided himself on removing from the chapel memorial tablets bearing such superstitious injunctions as *orate pro anima*. It may have been at this time that the inscription on the old brass commemorating Nicholas Metcalfe, still preserved in the modern ante-chapel, was partly obliterated.[1]

The royal supremacy was now in the hands of the Puritan masters of the country and they used it to their own ends. In 1644 the earl of Manchester was empowered to reform the university and in March he ordered the college to dismiss Dr Beale, the president and five of the seniority. A month later he installed John Arrowsmith as master, and fellows who would not subscribe to the Solemn League and Covenant were weeded out. In place of twenty-nine fellows ejected only twelve replacements were drafted in at first, being men from other colleges who 'could digest the Covenant'. The fellowship did not regain something like its normal strength until 1647, and there were new casualties in 1650 when a declaration of adherence to the constitution of the commonwealth was demanded. It is clear, however, that the college was not made Puritan without a struggle. Some of the older fellows avoided taking the Covenant and Henry Newcome, who came up in 1644, speaks of bitter feuds between old and new fellows.[2] His own tutor, Zachary Cawdrey, was removed from the proctorship in 1647 for using the prayer book and expressing royalist sympathies; and in the same year the anti-Puritan fellows felt strong enough to argue that the exclusion of those who refused the Covenant from college offices and fellowships was contrary to the statutes.

In the end, however, in Arrowsmith's later years and under his successor, Anthony Tuckney (1653–61), accommodation was reached with the new dispensation. Near-normality prevailed in fellowship elections and undergraduate entries were running slightly higher than in the 1630's. Some of the credit must go to the Puritan masters and to Tuckney in particular. He was zealous for the conversion of the Indians and for the propagation of the Gospel in America, but he was also a scholar himself and careful for scholarship and discipline in the college. He insisted that fellows must fulfil their teaching duties and that undergraduates should be diligent in their studies. A characteristic tale is told of him, that he 'was determined to choose none but scholars' for fellows of the college, 'adding very wisely: they may deceive me in their godliness; they cannot in their scholarship'.[1]

Tuckney's virtues did not save him when Charles II came home. He could accept the Restoration as such, but his chapel stall was empty when the use of the Book of Common Prayer was resumed. Further, some fellows ejected during the Puritan domination were now reinstated and others of like mind were imposed upon the college by royal mandate. The consequences appeared in February 1661, when the senior dean and twenty-nine fellows petitioned the king against the master on the grounds of his Puritanism, his absenting himself from chapel and his nursing of non-conformity in some part of the fellows.[2] By the end of that year Tuckney had been replaced by Peter Gunning and for some two centuries thereafter the college was a purely Anglican preserve. This fact alone did not abolish divisions and factions, but it did remove a great part of those religious grounds for controversy which had dominated collegiate life since the Reformation.

II

A time of storm and stress might seem, on the face of it, unfavourable to growth and development. Yet the college did grow: the number of men coming up rose from about thirty-three each year round 1550 to a peak of eighty in the late 1560's. After a fall to round forty-five in 1600, there was recovery once more to sixty or rather more in the 1630's and 1650's. Total numbers in residence in 1672 (when the annual entry was about sixty-four) are said to have been 373, compared with 152 in 1545.[3] Expanding numbers naturally imposed a strain upon accommodation, relieved in 1584–5 by converting the old infirmary into rooms for undergraduates (it was called 'the Labyrinth' in later days and was linked with the first court in 1636–7 by a covered passage passing round the east end of the chapel). Further space was found in 1588–9 by utilizing as living quarters a house called the Pensionary on the opposite side of St John's Street from the main gate. The latter accommodation was relinquished, however, and Metcalfe's little court was demolished when second court was erected. Completed in 1602, it was built by Ralph Symons of Westminster and Gilbert Wigge of Cambridge for £3600, of which £2760 was contributed by Mary, countess of Shrewsbury. Her statue, with a shield showing the arms of Talbot and Cavendish impaled, is to be seen above the gateway in the tower at the west end of the court, where it was placed in the reign of Charles II.

The new court had some features worthy of note. By contrast with the first court the staircases ran right up to the garret rooms on the top floor, which in the older buildings were accessible only through fellow's rooms on the floors below. The greater freedom which this allowed to undergraduates may well explain why, in the period of Puritan domination, something we may call a patrol of fellows was deemed necessary by nighttime to supervise the conduct of junior members. The most outstanding feature of the court, however, was the panelled long gallery with its remarkable plaster ceiling which was added to the master's accommodation. Now the combination room, it was originally a good deal longer than it is today. The present small combination room was taken off, probably in the mid-eighteenth century; and for a time the whole gallery was partitioned into a number of rooms, the other divisions being taken out when the master moved into the new lodge in 1865. Earlier, the gallery was curtailed to accommodate the staircase and vestibule of the new library built in 1623–5. The original dimensions of the room can still be discerned by tracing the plaster ceiling from the combination room right through to the library.

The new library, erected in the last days of James I, has continued to serve that purpose and was the first component of a third court. It cost £3000, of which about two thirds was provided by John Williams, bishop of Lincoln and Lord Keeper of the Privy Seal, formerly a sizar and fellow of the college. His biographer calls the building 'the chief Minerval which he bestowed upon the society' that had been 'the nurse of his hopeful breeding'; and his mark is still upon it in the initials I.L.C.S. (Johannes Lincolniensis, Custos Sigilli) which are best seen from the river, and in his arms, impaled with those of the see of Lincoln, set above the entrance doorway to the upper library. Their position reminds us that, originally, the ground floor of the building was occupied by rooms designed for the fellows and scholars whom Williams also endowed (in the event inadequately); and that the library was, until the nineteenth century, on the first floor only. Apart from necessary repairs from time to time and the heightening of the lower cases in the eighteenth century, its general appearance has altered little since Williams came down from his palace at Buckden in 1628 to inspect the outcome of his generosity. One feature taking us back almost to Williams's time is the compartments with doors on the larger cases, containing catalogues of c. 1685 pasted over others which date from about 1640.[1]

New buildings made more room, but high numbers still occasioned a good deal of crowding. Bishop Williams, for example, envisaged the provision of two rooms only for his four scholars (though his fellows were each to have a room to themselves); and D'Ewes implies that even a fellow commoner might have to share his chamber.[2] At first, indeed, chambers seem to have been allotted only to fellows, those on the ground floor to junior fellows and those above to the more senior. The latter were larger than the modern sets, for they included the garrets on the second floor as well as the first-floor accommodation. It was for this reason that, in first court, the main staircases (as may still be seen in B staircase) went not further than the first floor. Each unit, moreover, was a warren of accommodation for the pupils to whom a fellow acted as tutor. Tenants of first-floor chambers not only quartered men in the garrets: even on the lower floors 'we read of the "great bed" of the tutor and "truckle beds" in the same chamber. Partitions, in almost every corner where light can be obtained are erected to form "studies" about six feet square. The set of rooms over the butteries had six studies, four on one side, two on the other.' We are still a very long way from the nineteenth-century norm of a set for every man.[3]

All the same, there was a little more spaciousness after 1602. We begin to hear of scholars being allotted chambers which they might arrange to

II. THE UPPER LIBRARY, LOOKING EAST

share with others or another, and some fellow commoners, as we shall see, might be afforded quite princely accommodation. New amenities, too, were being provided. A tennis court was built in 1573 on the north side of the site of second court and moved across the river when that court was constructed. A bowling green was laid out on the northern part of what is now the Wilderness, a property acquired from the town in 1610; and it was connected with the college by a 'long walk' lined with trees. The creation and landscaping of the college Backs had begun.[1]

Growing numbers and additions to the fabric were made possible, in part at least, by the fact that the college continued to attract new benefactors. Second court and the library are memorials, in great part, to the generosity of the countess of Shrewsbury and of John Williams, and there were many others who added to the corporate funds of the college. The number of fellowships, it is true, increased only from forty-four in 1545 to fifty-two in the mid-seventeenth century; but at least thirty-six new scholarships were endowed during the same period, as well as a good number of exhibitions designed to give somewhat smaller assistance to needy students. There were also other benefactors who augmented existing foundations in order to offset the rise in the cost of living during a century of inflation. Among them was numbered Lord Burghley, who transferred a rent-charge to the college in order to increase from 7d. to 1s. the weekly allowance of the foundress's scholars for their commons.[2]

The fall in the value of money, which called for Burghley's benefaction, also created a whole range of financial problems. In face of it, there was no change in the essential policy of the college. Almost the whole of its revenues continued to be drawn from land, and cash benefactions, as earlier, were invested in real property. The rate at which the college estates were expanding, however, slowed down, and this at a time when prices were rising steeply and when the college was having to find some part of the capital expenditure incurred in new building. As early as 1579 Howland was complaining to Burghley that 'our number already is over great for the receipt of our house and the living (for these days) very small';[3] and the steadily falling purchasing power of money made increasingly inadequate the emoluments, mostly fixed by statute, of master, fellows, college officers and scholars. In this situation there was resort to expedients which easily became irregularities. The lease of one of the college properties, at the latest from 1599, was assigned to the master, and Baker tells us that some of the fellows were similarly accommodated.[1] The advantage lay in the fact that, since the rents charged by the college were low, the beneficiary might sub-let at a profit; and thus revenue which the college ought to have received for corporate purposes was diverted into the pockets of individuals. The practice was checked after an appeal to the visitor, but in the meantime another method of supplementing fellows' incomes became increasingly common. The college at this time was acquiring, mainly by gift, a number of ecclesiastical benefices, but these were used as a sort of pension fund to provide for those who vacated their fellowships on marriage or for other reason. On the other hand, it became customary to permit fellows to accept presentation to livings by patrons other than the college without relinquishing their fellowships. One consequence was that many fellows were partial absentees, and in this manner a pattern was established which persisted down to the nineteenth century.[2]

These palliatives, however, did not suffice in face of the great inflation of the century after 1540. It became quite essential to increase the payments made to fellows and scholars and, if that was to be made possible, it was necessary to make the college's estates yield more. This was not achieved, as was so often the case at the time, by 'rack-renting': on the contrary, the leasehold rents charged by the college retained on the surface a marvellous fixity. Yet estates were made to yield more. The college had long been used to leases involving some liveries in kind: Horningsea parsonage, for example, rendered 'two good and well brawned boars' and a holding in Barway a twenty-inch pike on Ash Wednesdays. As early as 1551, this principle was being extended: some college tenants were being asked to pay part of their rents in grain or, alternatively, in terms of the value of that amount of grain at current market prices; and legislation in 1580 obliged all tenants to pay one third of their rents in this manner. Since corn prices rose steadily the rents paid by tenants, though in appearance unchanged,

28

similarly rose. The resulting gain in revenue was distributed, partly in the form of gifts or *vales* to retiring fellows and partly as a 'dividend' to fellows and scholars to supplement their statutory allowances. In or around 1600, for example, the fellows received a bonus totalling £290 and the scholars one of £145.[1] The practice persisted and was recognized by the statutes of the nineteenth century. It is perpetuated down to this day in the payments to resident fellows under the name of *praeter*.

The 'corn-money', however, was soon eclipsed by another source of dividend. Tenants paid only one third of their rents at rates determined by the rising market value of corn and the balance was apt to remain unchanged over long periods. Rents, in consequence, were still 'beneficial' to tenants at a time of rising agricultural profits; and they were not unwilling, therefore, to pay periodic capital sums (called fines) for the renewal or reversion of leases. The manors of Higham and Lilliechurch alone were the subject of no less than six such payments between 1614 and 1657, from which the college received in all £1900. At first revenue from this source was used for special college purposes or for the payment of *vales*, but from 1629 it was also employed to pay periodic dividends to the master and fellows. The practice became regular and annual after 1645, and the dividend turned into an emolument far higher than the old statutory emoluments. Ultimately, to all intents, it replaced them. Thus the danger was avoided that inflation would eat into the standard of living of the fellows. It is even arguable that the general good of the college was sacrificed to concern on this point. Dividends absorbed almost the whole of the surpluses created by improvements in estate management and left little over for investment with an eye to the future. Some of the financial problems of later times had their origin in this tendency.

III

Significant changes in the inner life of the college are, by their nature, harder to delineate. The statutes of Henry VIII and Elizabeth, if we leave aside certain changes which the Reformation made necessary, suggest that little had altered since the times of Bishop Fisher; and the fact that the

Elizabethan statutes, with few and slight modifications, governed the college for nearly three centuries would seem to imply a positive immobility. The implication, as we shall see, is fallacious in many important respects, but there were things which changed slightly or slowly. The college in the seventeenth century, for example, was still a relatively youthful community. Of ninety-eight undergraduates who came up in the years 1630–1,[1] two were only thirteen years old. They were somewhat exceptional, but three-fifths of those admitted were seventeen or younger. Men also became fellows comparatively young (the average age in 1635–7 was below twenty-two) and retained their fellowships on the average only about twelve years. Even the seniors were not excessively venerable.[2] In the years 1570–81 they normally attained that station about eight years after they had been elected fellows. At this point, the noted Puritan, John Knewstub, was only twenty-eight, while Thomas Leach was thirty-two. In the seventeenth century, fellows might have to wait somewhat longer for seniority; but, as the practice of holding livings in plurality with fellowships spread, the titular seniors were often absent and their duties were performed by deputies. The latter were chosen from men less senior, so that the government of the college still continued in the hands of relatively young men. Nor should it be forgotten that William Whitaker was only forty-seven when he died, by which time he had been master for nearly nine years.

Lack of change in some directions did not preclude great and significant changes in others—changes which may have been pre-figured in earlier times, but which only worked themselves out in the days of Elizabeth and the early Stuarts. There are pointers to some of them in the pages of the college admission register, which was begun in 1630. It shows that, on the average in the period 1630–60, about five noblemen and fellow commoners, twenty-two pensioners and twenty-seven sizars were admitted every year. Sizars, in other words, constituted about half the body of undergraduates and, in return for some service to fellows and fellow commoners, obtained part at least of the cost of their maintenance and tuition and sometimes some emolument as well. A proportion of pensioners, too, were assisted by the awards of scholarships and exhibitions. The college, in fact, was still discharging in a notable manner the duty which Fisher had laid upon it to provide education, other things being equal, for boys from relatively poor homes. Some of them made good use of this start in life. John Williams, builder of the library, came up as a sizar. He went on to be, not only Lord Keeper and bishop of Lincoln, but eventually archbishop of York. Most, of course, did not rise so high. The normal destiny of a sizar or poor scholar was a parochial living, but in that respect, too, the college was fulfilling Fisher's intention.

The admission register, however, can be made to tell us a little more than this, for it provides information about the parentage of those who came to the college. Nearly a third of those who came up in the three decades after 1630 were sons of farmers, artisans and so forth—clearly, for the most part, men drawn from the less wealthy sections of the community. Even the 7 per cent who were sons of mercantile families and the 21 per cent who were sons of professional men (mainly clergymen) must often have had backgrounds of no great affluence. On the other hand, as we have seen, half of those who entered the college did so as pensioners or fellow commoners, though some of the former would become scholars in due course. Clearly, however, these categories of students seem somewhat more prominent than Fisher had envisaged. Again, about two-fifths of those who came up in the years 1630–60 were sons of noblemen or landed gentlemen. If they were younger sons, it is true, they might well be destined for the church or one of the other professions, so that Fisher's intentions would not thereby be frustrated. But not all were younger sons and the high proportion of gentlemen's sons in the seventeenth-century college appears to be a change of the greatest moment.

It was a change which came about amid a good deal of controversy in the times of the Tudors,[1] when the old medieval pattern of a gentleman's education (which had been basically military in character) was found wanting by Renaissance standards. Sir Thomas Elyot, Thomas Starkey, Nicholas Bacon and Sir Humphrey Gilbert all produced blue-prints for the new age, but all alike were unconcerned with the universities which were for 'youth determined to the spirituality'. Fisher and Latimer and Cranmer were here at one with them and so was Thomas Lever, who raised his voice—and it was no still, small voice—against rich men's sons who crept into colleges and usurped places and emoluments which ought to be devoted to the training of clerks. Ascham, too, for all his recognition of the fact that the college sent out men trained to serve the commonwealth, bemoaned the presence in the Cambridge of the 1540's of wealthy undergraduates in excessive numbers.[1] But powerful forces were at work to make these traditionalist views out of date. A more complex system of government called at every level for what Ascham called *apti et instructi viri*, men educated in the new humanist learning which professed to instil virtue and wisdom and to develop the talents of the whole man. William Cecil, in 1559, went so far as to suggest that the nobility ought to be compelled to bring up their sons to learning and that one third of college scholarships should be reserved for the sons of poorer gentlemen.[2] His own training at St John's, a precocious home of Renaissance education, perhaps formed him in this view; and he had been preceded in that college by Sir John Cheke and by Sir Thomas Wyatt, a diplomat as well as a poet. He was followed there by Sir Thomas Hoby and a whole galaxy of peers, including Strafford, Falkland and Fairfax who, between them, personified so many of the political attitudes of Stuart England. It was not without reason that, in 1606, St John's was described as '*omni exceptione majus; not inferior to any college for the bringing up of young gentlemen*'. There are reputed to have been as many as thirty-eight fellow commoners in residence at once in Whitaker's time, though this would be somewhat above the average of the next two generations.[3]

Other influences than this, of course, helped to determine the composition of the college. New scholarships and the place of St John's in common estimation drew undergraduates to it from all over England and quite notably from Wales—a contrast to its marked northern orientation in early days. Particular connections were established with certain schools, those with Sedbergh and Pocklington going back almost to the beginning, but also including Shrewsbury and to a lesser extent Rivington and

Aldenham; in all of them the college had certain rights in the appointment of headmasters. The seventeenth century also saw the establishment of the Johnson, Munsteven and Spalding exhibitions, creating links with Oakham, Uppingham, Oundle, Peterborough and Bury St Edmund's.[1] Still, the great matter of the time was a growing influx of gentlemen's and noblemen's sons. It was this, in combination with the operations of the royal supremacy, which made the college more secular in purpose, composition and outlook than ever Bishop Fisher had designed it to be.

Some of the results are obvious enough. Connections with the most influential strata of English society were strengthened and diversified. That helped to lengthen the roll of the college's benefactors; but it also made St John's part of 'the Tudor and Stuart system of patronage'. Fathers who had been there were anxious for their sons to follow them; and, if they were successful men, they might manage to achieve this end even though their sons were not particularly promising material. Thus a Johnian bishop of Chichester in 1604 sought entry for his boy,

being yet raw and not so forward as I could wish. I have long kept him at his books, but his conceit and apprehension is slow, his memory frail and his mind not so devout to study…unless by strict discipline he be held and spurred thereunto. I do not expect he should prove any great clerk…but my desire is that he should add something to what he hath, that he may prove fit for civil company and for some purpose in the commonweal.

Perhaps despite his father's honesty the young man was soon in residence and chosen a foundress's scholar. Parents might canvas for more than places: some asked for scholarships (one expressing the hope that 'my wild and rude carriage in time past shall not be argument to disgrace my child or keep him back from preferment') and others even for fellowships. One father in 1617 requested that a younger might succeed an elder brother as fellow, 'as the misery of my nine children yet unprovided for and my much cumbered and distressed estate doth require'. In this instance, however, the college did not concur, perhaps discouraged by the fact that the elder son, while holding his fellowship, had been cast into gaol for debt.[2]

In this last case, too, a deaf ear was turned to the countess of Shrewsbury and the duke of Buckingham, whose support had been enlisted to give added weight to parental pleading. The backing by influential men or women of candidates for fellowships or scholarships was a pressure to which the college was continuously subjected. A bishop of London wrote (and not unsuccessfully) asking a fellowship for a Sidney man, and offered the master a consideration in return: 'ask a prebend of me for your friend'; a dean of Lincoln sought a scholarship for the son of a 'religious knight' and hinted that the father might do Owen Gwyn some service; even the great Francis Bacon was dragged in to back two applicants for fellowships, though his knowledge of them seems only to have been second-hand. Many fellows were also imposed upon the college by royal mandate under the early Stuart kings, and most of them were the clients of patrons who chose to work through the court rather than approach the college direct. These operations helped to transform the character and notion of a fellow-ship. It came to be regarded, not so much as an opportunity for advanced training in theology, but as part of the proprietary system, a fee simple for the devolution of which a present incumbent might even make his own arrangements. We read in 1622 that 'Mr Young...is willing...to resign his fellowship to his kinsman and friend;...only he is desirous to be beforehand assured that his resignation will be accepted for him to whom he intends it, otherwise he is resolved not to part with his fellowship on any terms, he having no other end but to pleasure a friend'. This is a far cry from the intent of the fellowship statutes of Bishop Fisher or Queen Elizabeth.[1]

IV

The changes rooted in the external relations of the college had parallels within it. Sons of noblemen and gentlemen might well expect to live a life somewhat different from the quasi-monastic existence of Fisher's poor scholars. They might expect, too, conditions less rigorous than did the 'poor, godly, diligent students' of whom Thomas Lever has left so vivid a picture. The latter rose between four and five in the morning, kept chapel between five and six, then studied until ten, when they dined on 'a penny piece of beef among four, having a few porridge made of the broth of the same beef with salt and oatmeal and nothing else'. After dinner, they returned to study until five o'clock supper, which was 'not much better than their dinner'; then back again to study until nine or ten when, being without fires, they were 'fain to walk or run up and down for half an hour to get a heat on their feet when they go to bed'.[1]

There continued to be, as we have seen, many sons of poor men in the college: they must have lived frugally and some helped themselves through their university courses by undertaking vacation work (road-making round Cambridge, jobs at Stourbridge fair or harvesting in the surrounding countryside).[2] On the other hand, there were many who lived in a very different state. It was said that a fellow commoner at the beginning of the seventeenth century, without taking account of the cost of his clothes, bedding and furniture, required at least £64 a year for his maintenance. This was a sum four times the master's statutory stipend and one high enough to persuade the poet Herrick to move from St John's to less costly quarters as a pensioner of Trinity Hall. There were also a few whose expenses must far have exceeded this relatively modest figure. When the earl of Arundel proposed to send his two sons to the college in 1624, each was to be attended by a groom of his chamber; and they were to be accompanied by three gentlemen, each in turn with a servant. To accommodate this party the earl asked for five chambers; and he proposed to send with it two more gentlemen attendants, a footman and a stable groom who might be lodged in the town. Another parent, Sir Peter Frechevile, even made a proposition that his son should come into residence with his private tutor, a Trinity man, and that the college might wish to facilitate the arrangement by electing the latter a fellow. It did not so wish.[3]

Not every undergraduate of this sort was quite so diligent as Lever's poor, godly students had been. William Cavendish (later duke of Newcastle) is said to have displayed a disinclination for study and a devotion to sport; and Burghley's grandson, William Cecil, did not mince words when writing to his father. 'I never was out of love with my book, knowing learning to be a necessary and an excellent quality in any gentleman. For

3-2

my staying here, it must be as long as your lordship thinks good, but if your lordship do leave it to mine own choice I could be very well content to go from hence as soon as might be.' William Cecil, it is true, was very young at this time (apparently only about fifteen), and this youthfulness was characteristic of many of the sprigs of nobility in the college, as it might be of other undergraduates. Indeed, if proportion is to be retained, it may have to be admitted that 'the real school for the quality was in London: the Inns of Court'; that if such men came to a university, they did so young and moved on, still young, to their Inn; and that perhaps there was a feeling that 'not to be in London was to be out of life', with the result that 'Oxford and Cambridge fall into place as a preparatory school for London'.[1]

For all that, sons of gentlemen and noblemen did come to the college and in considerable numbers. Their presence may help to explain the provision of sporting facilities like the tennis court and the bowling green, the playing of football on Sheep's Green which D'Ewes recorded, and the recreation which 'learned masters and bachelors' allowed themselves in the form of running, leaping, pitching the bar and other like sports. Rich men's sons were perhaps a little less likely to have been so prominent in another extra-curricular activity for which the college had some reputation. A bishop of Carlisle, thanking the college for having elected his son a fellow in 1620, numbered among the latter's qualifications 'his skill in music and towardliness to act a part in comedies and tragedies'. He went on to say that, during his own time at Christ's (1579–96), St John's had excelled all other colleges in this 'kind of scholarly exercise'. The years he spoke of were near enough to the time of the St John's Parnassus plays—the peak of a tradition which went back to the 1520's and which was specifically recognized by the 1545 statutes, with their provision that each fellow shall be chosen in turn Lord of Christmas and their assumption that entertainments, comedies and tragedies written by him or by other members of the college will be regularly performed. Perhaps a decline had set in by 1613, when the college put on a comedy to entertain James I. An observer noted that it 'proved but a lean argument and, though it were larded with pretty shows at the beginning and end, and with somewhat too broad a speech for such a presence, yet it was still dry'.[1]

It must not be supposed, however, that the college was no more than a place for play-acting and for rich men's sons to live in idleness. Lord Falkland, it is true, confessed that he brought little learning from St John's, but he added that 'the fruits are unproportionate to the seed-plot';[2] and D'Ewes showed that even a fellow commoner might be a serious student. It is true, too, that a good number of men took no degrees, but that did not necessarily mean that they got no education. In this respect, college and university statutes are a very imperfect guide. The official academic curricula, indeed, may have narrowed rather than expanded after the mid-sixteenth century. An exception was something of a revival in the study of Roman law at the end of the century, leading to the exemption from the statutory obligation to take orders accorded by Charles I to two fellows of the college who would engage themselves in studying the law. That apart, in the courses which led to degrees, Greek and Hebrew may have lost a little ground to the basic studies of philosophy and theology and, in Elizabethan times, there was something of a reaction against Bishop Fisher's patronage of medical studies at St John's. The statutes of 1580 limited to two the number of medical fellows who were exempted from the obligation to be ordained, and this seems to be connected with a petition from the college demanding that divines should be preferred to physicians in the elections of senior fellows. Science in general was not more favoured than medicine. Matthew Robinson, who made an adventurous journey from the north in war-time to come up in 1645, reckoned physics (interpreted, perhaps, with less than modern strictness, as comprehending anatomy, astronomy, meteorology and natural history) among those 'jejune studies' which required not more than 'one month's enquiry'. It has also to be admitted that William Gilbert, author of *De Magnete*, fellow in 1561 and Linacre lecturer, did his original work after he left Cambridge. It was not there, where almost the only staple was Aristotle's *Physics*, that he learned (save in a negative way) to verify things with his own eyes and to put his trust in 'reliable experiments and not in the opinions of ordinary professors and philosophers'. Nor did mathematics particularly flourish. Henry Billingsley went down in the early 1550's without a degree and published his English translation of Euclid only in 1570; and Henry Briggs, who developed Napier's discovery of logarithms, found real outlet for his gifts as reader in geometry at Gresham House in London (1596–1619) and later as Savilian professor at Oxford. Mathematics would have their day in Cambridge, but that day was not yet.

Yet for all this it would be wrong to deduce that there was mere stagnation or even retrogression in educational scope and method. The university was training a greater diversity of men for a greater diversity of roles in English life; and this made differences in practice if not in the statutory rules which professed to govern practice. The long-drawn course of theological instruction which Fisher's statutes envisaged ceased to be the sole norm. More men, if they took a degree at all (and many did not), went down after completing their B.A.; and from 1608 three additional years of continuous residence were no longer even a nominal requirement for proceeding M.A. The academic course, in other words, even for those destined for the priesthood, was assuming its modern duration. Again, the tendency evident earlier to make university instruction, the 'public lectures', merely an appendage to college instruction, continued and became more pronounced. For this reason the college's staff of thirteen lecturers and examiners was raised to fifteen by the Henrician and Elizabethan statutes and, without benefit of statute, to twenty by 1647. The educational autonomy of the college, destined to endure almost into the present century, was becoming more complete.[1]

Not less significant was the growing importance of the college tutor. All fellows performed this office to a varying number of pupils, but the more senior and successful naturally gathered more about them than did their juniors. As early as 1565 we find William Fulke with at least a dozen pupils. Manifold duties were involved, for a tutor was held responsible for his pupil's conduct. One father in 1616 adjured his son's tutor to have a care that the young man 'avoid the company of tobacco-takers, drinkers and swaggerers' and desired that he would have 'a special care of him, as well for his conversation as his learning'. If the roots of this responsibility are to be found in Fisher's statutes, the influx of gentlemen's sons into the college probably helped to develop the tutorial office: for fathers of rank would be concerned that their sons should be under good guidance at the university and the college that its reputation should be enhanced by honouring that trust. Under the Puritan masters, indeed, the day was always rounded off with prayers in the tutors' chambers.

This was only the beginning of a tutor's duty. He saw to the accommodation of his pupils, sometimes in his own chamber. He was financially responsible for them, for which reason we find D'Ewes' tutor, Richard Holdsworth, visiting his pupil's father to collect certain arrears. Above all, however, he assumed an increasing responsibility for the education of his charges. One father wrote to Owen Gwyn asking that a tutor be appointed for his son 'who will strictly hold him in obedience, diligently read unto him and keep him in continual exercise', adding that 'if his tutor bestow on him care and pains extraordinary, my thankfulness and stipend to him will be more than ordinary'. Richard Holdsworth amply fulfilled this office towards Simonds D'Ewes. He read with him logic, ethics, physics, Aristotle's *Economics* and *Politics* and Florus's *Roman History*; 'besides, in his private chamber at nights, he read exceeding well upon Virgil's *Eclogues*'. Even college lectures and exercises were, to some degree, being thrust from the centre of the picture by tutorial instruction. The result was that the old statutory college teaching officers took the first steps towards their ultimate obscurity, and began to leave the field to tutors teaching privately and for personal emolument.

The tendency perhaps gave a new intensity to college teaching; but it also gave it new dimensions and enabled the college to make better provision for a more diverse body of undergraduates. It became possible, in fact, to superimpose upon the statutory curriculum, which was designed to produce trained theologians, other curricula which, even if they led to no degree, still provided genuine intellectual training. The relative breadth of territory covered is suggested by the course which Matthew Robinson set himself, for all his contempt of physics, when he came up to St John's.

'He fixed upon a settled resolve to study for seven hours per day at least: four of these hours he spent in philosophy, his morning study; the afternoon hours he devoted...to Greek and Latin poets,...history, geography, etc.', making up at night any time lost during the day through company or by exercises in the college and the schools.[1]

Even better illustration is to be found in the exercise of his office by D'Ewes' tutor, Richard Holdsworth, who later left St John's to become master of Emmanuel College. We have already seen his pupil at work with him upon Aristotle's *Politics* and Roman history; and if D'Ewes' own interests took him to Spenser's *Faerie Queen*, Guiccardini, Commines, Old English chronicles and the history of Columbus's voyages, perhaps we may infer that this was not in face of positive tutorial discouragement. Holdsworth has also left a manual of instructions for his pupils. It has much to say about method: the order of studies, what books should be thoroughly digested and what scanned, and how notes should be taken. Tutorial instruction is a serious, a professional matter. The content of his teaching is not less significant. Full provision is made for the subjects prescribed by the university for undergraduate study—rhetoric, logic and philosophy; and the work of preparation includes practice disputations in the tutor's rooms before proceeding to public exercises in college chapel or university schools. But he also adds ancient literature, ancient and modern history and universal geography to the undergraduate's curriculum; and towards those who do not intend to take a degree he is even more liberal. Their fare includes Burton's *Anatomy of Melancholy*, Erasmus's *Encomium Moriae*, More's *Utopia* and the poetry of Crashaw, Herbert and Buchanan.[2]

The Henrician and Elizabethan statutes, then, deceive us in giving too immobile a portrait of the late Tudor and early Stuart college. Secular forces worked a transformation in the Lady Margaret's school of theology, however much it still served that purpose and however much theological controversy dominated its internal affairs. The royal supremacy and the new aristocracy, gentry and men of affairs were real influences upon it. This was one of the consequences of the fact that academic learning had been accepted as 'a necessary and an excellent quality in any gentleman' and that St John's was 'not inferior to any college for the bringing up of young gentlemen'. It not only took in more fellow commoners and pensioners, more sons of noblemen, gentlemen and high government servants: it also trained more of its undergraduates for the world rather than for the priesthood. Even fellows might end in public service rather than a parish. Cheke and Ascham led the way and they were followed by other (if somewhat less notable) men. Ambrose Copinger was for a brief time rector of Buxhall, but he settled down in the end to be a country gentleman, represented Ludgershall in parliament and was knighted by James I; and Henry Hickman eventually made his career as a master in chancery and sat in parliament for Northamptonshire. Corresponding to these changes, which reflect a changing society, went others in the college's educational provision. The development of the tutorial system completed the process which made the college into a virtually autonomous teaching institution. At the same time, it gave new intensity and flexibility to the instruction it was capable of providing. Whatever the statutes might say or fail to say, it equipped itself to be a place for the bringing up of young gentlemen as well as to be a school of theology. For both reasons, at a time of religious controversy, political conflict and improvement in the arts of government, it was a force in English life.

III

THE UNREFORMED COLLEGE
(1661-1765)

THERE are striking contrasts between the history of the college in the
century before the Restoration and its history in the century which followed. A period of intense movement and fundamental changes was succeeded by an epoch which, in the college as in the university, was in many
respects one of stagnation. The spirit of Beale, too, triumphed over that of
Lever and Whitaker. St John's came to be, very soon after the Restoration,
the high Anglican and Tory college *par excellence* in Cambridge, a character
it did not lose until well down into the nineteenth century. There is no
necessary correlation between this atmosphere and a tendency towards stagnation, as was demonstrated after 1765 when Anglican and Tory sentiment
proved not incompatible with academic forwardness. For a century, however, these two characteristics went hand in hand, which makes it appropriate to begin the college's post-Restoration history with some account
of how new masters laid the ghosts of Arrowsmith and Tuckney.

I

We have already seen how old fellows restored, and new fellows intruded
by the king's mandate, got rid of Anthony Tuckney. The royal supremacy
also played a part in making his successor. On 18 June 1661, Charles II
wrote to the fellows 'to encourage you in those goodly thoughts you have
...to make choice of...Dr Gunning', and Dr Gunning duly became
master. It was intended that he should 'rout out the old leaven' and 'factious
and pernicious principles', a task for which he was well fitted. He had
been ejected by the Puritans from his fellowship at Clare and made master

of Corpus Christi College by royal mandate in 1660; he was 'strict in discipline and awful in his looks', and a man strong enough to impose upon St John's the character it was long to bear.[1] One outward and visible sign of his attitude was his concern for restoring something of Beale's régime in the college chapel. He had the organ rebuilt (perhaps for the first time with two manuals) and showed a continuous regard for the choir. In 1671, certain room rents in the new third court were assigned, in consideration of donations made to the building by Gunning and others, to the stipends of two counter-tenors, four trebles and a music master (it being assumed that some of the choristers might be undergraduates, since they could receive their stipends without prejudice to any scholarship emoluments to which they might be entitled). Gunning's will also refers in 1680 to 'the choir begun to be founded in St John's' and contained a legacy of £100 'for the better provision of male voices for the choir, whereby God's services may be more solemnly performed and decently sung'. There is little doubt that the history of the choir is continuous from this point, although for a time little is known of it—save that John Ambrose bequeathed half the tithes of Addingham (Cumberland) for its maintenance in 1681 and that the organist was given a gratuity in 1742 for entering the anthems in the college books.[2]

Long before Gunning made his will, however, he had resigned the mastership when he was promoted bishop of Chichester in 1670, moving thence to Ely in 1675. His successors, meantime, had continued his work. The next master was Francis Turner, who had been attracted from Oxford to Cambridge by friendship for Gunning and who was to end his career a deprived bishop for refusing the oath of allegiance to William III. Yet he was perhaps not entirely popular within the college, for he resigned in 1679 a few years before James II advanced him, first to the bishopric of Rochester and then (as Gunning's successor) to Ely. At St John's he was followed by Humphrey Gower, a man with a past to live down. His father had been a Puritan divine who, with others of like opinion, was employed in 1643 'to new-model a mongrel kind of church after their own fancies'; and he himself became a fellow of the college under Anthony Tuckney. These apparent disqualifications for advancement may have made his later conformity all the more enthusiastic. He became master of Jesus College under Gunning's patronage in 1679, but was translated from there to St John's in the same year (for this reason and for his severity he is 'the devil of Jesus' in Abraham de la Pryme's diary). His eminent suitability by this time he demonstrated in 1681 when he expressed, as the leader of a deputation from the university to the king at Newmarket, 'detestation of the late rebellions and factious practices and...well-instructed zeal for the church established'. There could be no doubt cast upon the purity of his royalism. 'We still believe and maintain that our kings derive not their titles from the people, but from God; that to Him only are they accountable; that it belongs not to subjects to create or censure, but to honour and obey their sovereign; who comes to be so by a fundamental, hereditary right of succession which no religion, no law, no fault or forfeiture can alter or diminish.'[1] Filmer, not Locke, was the guiding prophet of St John's and ultra-royalism was conjoined once more with high Anglicanism.

During Gower's long rule of thirty-two years, therefore, Gunning's work was rounded off; but, for all the former's impeccably royalist sentiments, where royalism and Anglicanism came into conflict it was Anglicanism which carried the day. The testing time came under James II, when the royal supremacy was used on behalf of Roman Catholics. Among the seven bishops imprisoned in the Tower in 1688 for opposing James's declaration of indulgence, three were Johnians: the former master, Francis Turner, lately so much in favour that he had been chosen to preach the king's coronation sermon, White of Peterborough and Lake of Chichester. Another Johnian, Thomas Smoult, made a fellow by royal mandate and later advanced to the Knightbridge chair of moral philosophy, was likewise a leader in the university's resistance to James's attempt, supported by the bullying of Judge Jeffreys, to secure a degree for a Benedictine monk.

Once James was across the water, however, and the danger to the church had passed, Tory sentiments came back into vogue. Francis Turner was by no means the only Johnian non-juror. In 1693 Gower received an order from the court of King's Bench to eject twenty of the fellows who had refused the oath of allegiance to William III and Mary. The master himself had taken the oath, and there may be justice in Cole's comment that 'he had a mastership, a canonry and a professorship' (the Lady Margaret chair of divinity) to lose. He was tender, none the less, to the non-jurors. He took no action on the mandate of the court and was himself indicted at the Cambridge assizes for his contempt. His defence is not without interest. A fellowship, he argued, was a freehold; and Magna Carta and many other statutes forbade a man to be put out of his freehold save by due process of law. This proposition, however, never came to trial, for the case against Gower ceased upon a technicality.[1] The non-jurors were not deprived until 1717, by which time fourteen of the original twenty had died or departed or conformed, although the rump had been joined by four new recruits. One of the originals who survived was Thomas Baker, the historian of the college and correspondent of many scholars. After 1717 he always inscribed his books *socius ejectus*, but his severance from the college was far from complete. He continued to reside in third court until the afternoon in 1740 when he was found lying in his rooms, his tobacco pipe broken by his side. He died within a few days, but marked his gratitude for the college's hospitality, which did not cease when the law of the land ended his fellowship, by leaving a wonderful collection of books to the library. They still enrich its shelves.[2]

The hermitage offered to Baker and the rest of the non-jurors is testimony to Tory and high Anglican sentiment in St John's; so was Ambrose Bonwicke's appreciation, when he came up in 1710, of the solemnity of its chapel services.[3] It was not, therefore, surprising that, when Gower died in 1711, he was followed by Robert Jenkin who had only seceded from the ranks of the non-jurors in that year. Thus the old ways were perpetuated even though times were changing; but on Jenkin's death in 1727 there were signs that former unanimity was breaking. For the first time for many years the mastership election was seriously contested and there was much jockeying among the five candidates before Robert Lambert won the day. His sympathies were clearly shown. He was the Tory candidate for the vice-chancellorship in 1729 and gained office by a single vote; but he lost it again in the following year to Dr Mawson of Corpus Christi

College, who stood in the Whig interest which was gathering strength in the university at large.[1] That fact, if no other, may have led some members of the college to wonder at the wisdom of defending lost causes.

Politics, indeed, were coming back to divide the college, a fact especially noticeable after the duke of Newcastle became chancellor of the university in 1748 and added it to the Whig empire of patronage. Even earlier, however, the effect had been felt in the mastership election which followed Lambert's death in 1735. John Newcome, who emerged successful from the contest, had stood against Lambert in 1727 and passed at least for a Whig. Not surprisingly the arch-Tory, William Cole, is severe towards him. He tells us that Newcome, in case it offended the Whigs, withdrew a dissertation he had written to preface Zachary Grey's edition of Butler's *Hudibras*; and that Newcastle was the master's 'great patron'. For this last suggestion there is this much support that, when Newcastle's success in winning the chancellorship was announced, Newcome 'pulled off his cap and flourished it round three or four times over his head'. There may be evidence, too, for his sentiments in the fact that the college subscribed £200 towards enlisting men for the king's service on the outbreak of the '45 rebellion; and also in the suggestion that, at least at first, the master 'was often made uneasy by the difference of his politics with those of his fellows'. Perhaps, had this been the sixteenth century, there would have been strenuous efforts to get rid of him; but in these new times, as even Cole has to admit, 'towards the latter end matters cooled'.

The truth may well be that tempers were no longer so warm as they had been, that a rigorous Toryism had become anachronistic and an impediment to securing the lucrative ecclesiastical preferment which was the crown of an academic career, and that there was more Whiggery in the college than a generation earlier. Whatever the reason may have been, Newcome had time, during a prefecture which lasted for thirty years, 'to model the college...according to his own system'.[2] His rule was by no means without achievement even if it lacked dramatic highlights. Some financial abuses, as we shall see, were rooted out. The chapel and hall were put in repair and firmer discipline was imposed upon the more unruly undergraduates. A good deal of concern was shown for the library: the books were rearranged, a new catalogue was made and such works were ordered as Stewart's *Antiquities of Athens*, Clarendon's *Letters* and Buffon's *Natural History*.[1] Newcome himself left sixty volumes to the college, mainly early editions of the classics handsomely bound in crimson morocco, which had probably been bought from the Harleian library. More than that, he left property to endow the first of the college prizes: it was to be bestowed yearly 'on the best moral philosopher that shall take his degree of bachelor of arts with good reputation'. The prize has continued to be awarded and to bear his name, and with his gift of books it ought not to be forgotten in estimating his concern for the well-being of the college as a place of education.

II

During the century after the Restoration, then, the college, although it was not unaffected by the stresses and strains of English political life, was more peaceful than it had been in most earlier generations. Relative calm, however, did not stimulate expansion. In the first two decades after 1660 the annual entry of undergraduates was running at around sixty-four, only very little above what it had been in the time of the Puritan masters. There-after it fell away until, between 1740 and 1760, it reached a low point of about thirty-two admissions yearly.[2] Before decline began, however, relatively high enrolments under Gunning and Turner again produced a demand for new buildings. The southern and western ranges of third court were constructed in 1669–73, the former incorporating an earlier building at its western end and being the first in the university planned to contain two rooms in thickness. The total cost was rather over £5000, of which about half was raised by an appeal to old members of the college: we find the earl of Rutland sending £10 with the observation that 'the widow's mite was received as well as the greater offerings'.[3]

Falling numbers made this the end of residential building until the nineteenth century. Furthermore, the fact that there were fewer under-graduates made it possible steadily to alleviate the excessively cramped conditions under which earlier generations had lived, though in Ambrose

Bonwicke's time at the beginning of the eighteenth century 'chums' might still share a chamber.[1] There were also a few improvements in other directions. In 1698 the college was in consultation with Christopher Wren about a stone bridge to link third court with the Backs. Wren provided a design and recommended that the new bridge should be so placed that it would prolong the axis of the three existing courts. The bridge was built eventually by Robert Grumbold in 1708–12, making some use of Wren's design but discarding his site: for it was placed where the old wooden bridge had been, continuing the line of the kitchen lane. Once again old members of the college, including 'silver-tongued' Anthony Hammond (who came up as a fellow commoner in 1685 and was M.P. for the university in 1698), contributed to the cost.[2] The landscaping of the Backs was likewise continued in the late seventeenth century, when their 'fine walks' and 'pretty bowling green' delighted Celia Fiennes; and again in the 1760's, when the Wilderness was bounded by a yew hedge and gravel was applied to the paths which led through the Backs to the fields beyond.[3]

These operations were on a smaller scale than those of the sixteenth and the nineteenth centuries, and small changes rather than great were likewise characteristic of the college's financial history. That is not to say that it failed to attract new and notable benefactions. In 1682 and 1686 Sarah, duchess of Somerset, gave lands (still in the ownership of the college) at March and Wootton Rivers to establish scholarships attached to Hereford, Marlborough and Manchester schools. In 1684 William Platt left to the college an estate in Kentish Town, and this legacy was used to endow fellowships and scholarships which had the particular advantage that they carried no restrictions as to a candidate's place of birth. Again, in 1710, George Baker (Thomas Baker's elder brother) gave £1300 to the college to establish exhibitions attached to Durham school, yet another connection which has persisted to this day.[4] In such ways the college's capital resources continued to grow, and by the eighteenth century not quite all of them were held in the form of real property. East India stock is mentioned in 1749, some of it being sold in 1750 and the proceeds put into three per cent annuities. In 1763 £2500 were invested in Old South Sea stock and two

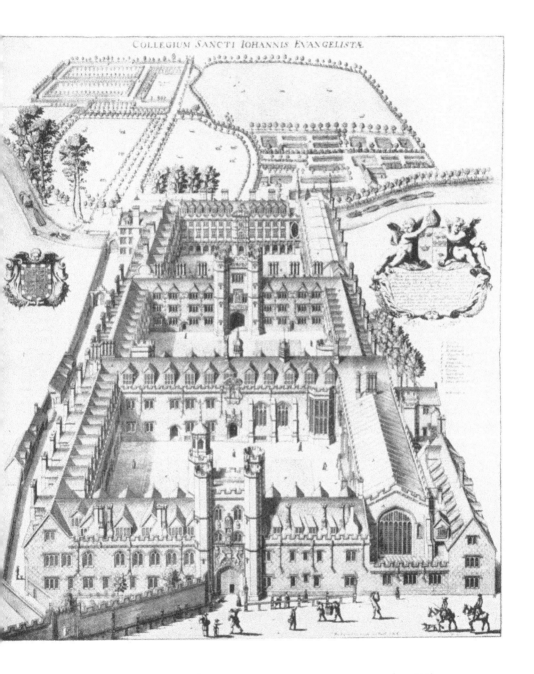

III. VIEW OF ST JOHN'S COLLEGE, BY DAVID LOGGAN (*c.* 1688)

years later a further £500 were put into similar securities.[1] In general, however, these holdings did not represent permanent investments: rather they were the method of holding balances until they were used or laid out upon real property. The base of the collegiate economy continued to be a territorial one.

In the management of its land the college was neither excessively sensitive nor quite insensitive to the winds of change. There were no alterations of principle. Tenants continued to pay relatively low rents; one third of those rents was expressed in terms of corn; and recompense for beneficial rents was still exacted in the form of periodic fines for renewals and reversions of leases. The level of fines, however, showed an upward tendency, in part because the value of land was rising and in part because the college increased the factor it used to calculate fines. By the mid-eighteenth century, too, some benefit was being felt from encouragement given to agricultural improvement. In 1761, for example, Marfleet was being enclosed. The college stimulated its tenants to co-operate, and to bear the costs of enclosure, by promising renewal of leases at the old rents. Those who did not co-operate were not to have their leases renewed and even those who did might clearly expect higher rents when their new leases eventually ran out.[2]

The effect of these policies was an increase in the external revenue of the college and new benefits accrued to the fellows in particular. It was possible in 1750 to increase the salaries of the deans and the steward by £10 a year; in 1756 to allow the fellows a penny a day apiece for greens;[3] and above all to increase the dividend paid to fellows from the fine money. The total distributed rose from around £450 yearly in the 1660's to £610 in the decade which began in 1700 and then to £1640 in the 1750's. In 1690 the master's share was £30, a senior fellow's £15 and a junior fellow's £10; during the 1750's a junior fellow's dividend rose quickly from £20 to £40 a year and his elders and betters gained proportionately. In this way a fellowship became a far more attractive proposition than it had been in most past times. To this rule there was one exception. The emoluments of the Platt fellows were fixed in 1684 at £10 yearly with an allowance for

4

49

rooms. At that time this was roughly what other fellows received, but the rise in the dividend paid to others turned the Platt fellows, for a hundred years or so after the mid-eighteenth century, into a depressed class.

If basic financial policy was conservative, there was still nothing essentially unsound about it. On the other hand, the management of the college's resources betrayed some typically eighteenth-century features. To begin with, accountancy had its anachronistic qualities, which were pilloried unmercifully by W. S. Powell, shortly after he became master, in 1769. The main accounts, as he pointed out, took no notice of the expression of a part of the rents for property in corn, a system already two centuries old. Rents appeared in them which had not been collected for a hundred years and nearly £1000 of rent did not appear at all, being dealt with in sub-accounts of their own. In brief, it was impossible to obtain from them any overall financial picture; or, to give the situation the more sinister interpretation which appealed to Powell, there was a deliberate attempt to ensure that the master and seniors 'might not easily perceive how fast the cash of the college was increasing nor the senior bursar be liable to be called upon for the balance of all his accounts at once'.

There were grounds for Powell's suspicions. He tells us that cash balances had become 'so considerable that the bursars were able to place £5000 or £6000 or more in public funds for their own emolument'— a manner of proceeding not unknown in higher places and one which would not have seemed strange to Sir Robert Walpole. All the same, it made the senior bursar's office at once attractive and risky. Its attractiveness became evident in 1747, when Dr Fogg resigned but promised to vote for Dr Green as his successor provided the latter allowed Fogg to retain for a further year the money he had invested in the funds. The risks appeared during the bursarship of Dr John Taylor (1750–8). He lost nearly £600 of college money as the result of a fall in the stocks and in the end nearly half of this had to be written off. The outcome was a college order forbidding bursars to invest college balances on their own accounts and increasing the bursar's salary by £30 yearly to encourage more modern standards of financial probity.[1]

There is a footnote to the tale of the college's financial policy in the century after the Restoration. As we have seen, fellows (apart from two engaged in the study of medicine and two others studying law) were under a statutory obligation to assume priests' orders within six years of proceeding M.A.; and all without exception had to relinquish their fellowships if they married. The latter rule made it likely that most fellows would wish to retire later, if not sooner; and the former suggested an appropriate way of providing for them. Something analogous to a pension fund was created by accumulating benefices in the college's gift to which retiring fellows were collated. Ecclesiastical benefices owned by the college were notably augmented during this period. In all some twenty-seven benefices were acquired by gift or purchase and, in addition, Richard Hill in 1717 obliged his heirs to present fellows to five Norfolk livings in the gift of his family. All in all, the provision for fellows matrimonially inclined or desirous of retirement became moderately adequate. College livings were offered to fellows in strict order of seniority and it may well have been the custom in the eighteenth century, as it was almost to the end of the nineteenth, for a vacancy in one of them to be brought to the notice of the seniors by the butler proclaiming the fact publicly in hall.[1]

III

All this, however, has taken us to the end of a fellow's life-cycle.[2] If we go back to the beginning we find that, at the opening of the eighteenth century as at the opening of the seventeenth, about two fifths of those elected fellows had originally come up as sizars. A fellowship, in other words, was within the ambition of the poor boy of talent and John Green, like his predecessor John Williams, rose through a sizarship and a fellowship to eventual eminence as bishop of Lincoln. A man might hope to get his fellowship when aged from twenty-two to twenty-four: a little later than in the seventeenth century because the average age of coming up to college had risen to seventeen and a half by 1715 and to eighteen by 1760. Having been chosen into a fellowship, the tendency was to keep it rather longer than in earlier days, the average rising to somewhere in the region of fifteen years. In so far as the tendency was a general one, it is likely to have been associated with the upward trend of the fellows' dividend and of the fees which could be earned by tutors and assistant tutors. A fellowship, in fact, carried the opportunity to receive emoluments attractive enough to make men cling to them.

At the same time, the average length of tenure was pushed up by the fact that a section of the fellows, at the cost of eschewing matrimony or deferring it, were holding fellowships much longer than had been customary in the past. It was from this group, of course, that the seniority was recruited, and in the mid-eighteenth century a man seldom attained the rank of senior until he was somewhat over forty. It was then normal for him to remain a senior for eight or nine years longer, that is, until he was around the age of fifty. As in earlier times, it is true, some seniors performed their office by deputy (three out of eight were doing so in 1750),[1] but the deputies were of like age with their principals. Perhaps this increased venerability of the seniority has some bearing on the caution and conservatism of college policy at this time; but whatever truth there may be in such a supposition, at least it may have been indirectly a result of the college's own policy to increase the number of livings in its gift. Some of them were of considerable value: Ufford-cum-Bainton, Brandesburton and Meppershall were all valued at £200 a year and Layham at £240, which were good sums in that age. They were, therefore, prizes for which it was worth growing older.

There was further encouragement. The time of waiting could be rendered not unprofitable. It continued to be permissible for a fellow, without forfeiting his fellowship, to hold benefices to which he had been presented by patrons other than the college. Only a few of the seniors in the years 1750–65 had forborne to take advantage of this dispensation: the elder John Taylor (the errant senior bursar of 1758 and a law fellow who only took orders late in life); William Heberden, who was a practising physician; and some four others. The remaining seventeen seniors had all received ecclesiastical preferment: some, indeed, were already pluralists and when at last they got a college living, that often merely added to their pluralism. Zachary Brooke, a senior fellow 1757–65, is not altogether un-typical of this group. He became a fellow in 1739 and vicar of Ickleton (Cambs) in 1744. In 1764 he was presented by the Hill family to the rectories of Forncett St Mary and Forncett St Peter in Norfolk; and a year later he became Lady Margaret professor of divinity and married, thus relinquishing his fellowship. He still retained all his livings, however, and they were 27 miles apart as the crow flies, prompting the observation that 'by the help of Dr B's crow any might hold preferment in the church'. It ought to be added that his professorship was no impediment to any pastoral duties to which he may have been inclined. It was justly called a 'valuable sinecure', for he never lectured. In that he was merely following magisterial example: his predecessor had been Dr Newcome and he, too, had 'care-fully avoided any hungry sheep which might be waiting to be fed'.[1]

Thus livings and fellowships, like professorships, easily became sinecures or quasi-sinecures. Fellows might neglect their benefices for their fellow-ships as Michael Burton did, for he resided continuously in Cambridge during the eleven years he was vicar of Hathersage in Derbyshire. Even retirement from a fellowship did not necessarily make a man into a resident pastor: Samuel Johnson, presented by the college in 1775 to Freshwater rectory in the Isle of Wight, lived and died in Yorkshire where he served on the commission of the peace. Conversely, fellows might be virtually non-resident in college. Stuart dispensations perhaps helped to ingrain this pattern, as when Charles II permitted one fellow to accompany the English ambassador to Russia and James II allowed another to go abroad as tutor to the earl of Rochester's son. In similar manner, many things took Matthew Prior away from his duties in the college. Elected a fellow in 1688 and a senior fellow in 1707, he was also appointed Linacre lecturer, for which office his sole qualification would seem to be 'the mirth and consequently health-giving character of his poems'. From 1697, however, he was much engaged in public service, including the representation of East Grinstead in parliament and of the English government at Paris in 1712 during the negotiations which led up to the Treaty of Utrecht.[2] Less notable preoccupations also entailed non-residence. Edward Beresford, fellow from 1725 to 1752, was rector of Tarporley in Cheshire: he died there after being for ten years so crippled with gout that he could not leave his room. Not surprisingly, he was one of those represented by a deputy at meetings of the seniority in 1750. William Heberden, too, left Cambridge for London in 1748 or 1749, but he only resigned his fellowship in 1752 when it was clear that he could support himself from the practice of medicine; and Joseph Cardale lived mainly at his Leicestershire rectory of Newbold Verdon between 1743 and 1759, at which point he came back to the college as senior bursar without feeling any necessity to resign his benefice.

It may not be surprising that many fellows of this sort were not scholars of note even if few of them died, as Cole said John Wilson did, 'like a hog, as he and his wife had lived'. Some, it is true, published works of theology or sermons—including John Cradock (later archbishop of Dublin), John Ross (later bishop of Exeter), William Weston, Zachary Brooke and Samuel Ogden. Ogden's sermons, indeed, were considered excellent by William Cole even though they were 'exceeding short', and presumably it was the former rather than the latter quality of them which attracted a 'thronged audience' to hear him at the Round Church in Cambridge. Others, however, were less kind than Cole. Another fellow of St John's said of Ogden that he used much scriptural quotation 'merely to lengthen out his short discourses', and Dr Johnson failed apparently to appreciate their merits. Boswell recommended them 'both for neatness of style and subtility of reasoning', moving Johnson to declare: 'I should like to read all that Ogden has written'. So the sermons went with them on their expedition to the Hebrides and Johnson took them to his room one night in Edinburgh. However, 'he did not stay long, but soon rejoined us in the drawing room', and they proved no more attractive at Aberdeen. Johnson, we are told, sometimes took up Ogden 'and glanced at it, but threw it down again'. Still, it is doubtless hard to preach to all men's tastes and Ogden at least had been pleasing to some.[1]

Some few, however, have somewhat larger achievements to their names. William Salisbury, after he retired to Moreton rectory, published a work on grammar and a translation of Bullet's *History of the Establishment of Christianity*, to which he appended notes and certain strictures upon Gibbon; the elder John Taylor (not the peccant bursar, but Dr Johnson's 'Demosthenes Taylor') devoted himself to scholarship for thirty years, edited the Attic orators and published much else on the classics besides; and William Ludlam was a prolific author on mathematical subjects, astronomy and mechanics, his works including essays on church organs and on a newly constructed balance for woollen manufacture. If these men were somewhat exceptional, perhaps there is only one name which stands right out from the ruck. William Heberden the elder became a fellow in 1731 and a medical fellow (and therefore exempted from the necessity of taking orders) in 1734. For ten years he lectured on physic in Cambridge and laid the foundations for his rationalization of pharmacology and *materia medica*. His best work and writing, however, like William Gilbert's, was done after he left Cambridge for a London practice, wherein he garnered the material for his commentaries in the form of notes taken at the bedside, which were always being revised in the light of new cases. His world was very different from the Cambridge medical world of the eighteenth century, in which two men held the regius professorship for ninety-three years between them and published nothing. Heberden's qualities, at least, were not quite unrecognized in St John's. Some abiding affection on his part is indicated by the fact that he left his *materia medica* cabinet, still preserved in the library, to the college; but there is also more positive testimony to a regard for him on the college's part. Erasmus Darwin, as an undergraduate in the years 1752–3, copied his *Introduction to the Study of Physic* and his *Doctrine of the Pulse* into a notebook to which some friends appended the remark: 'Damn you, Darwin, you have spelt a thousand words wrong, you son of a whore'; and in 1764 the college determined that it would send to Heberden a collar of brawn each Christmas time.[1]

There was a further consequence of much non-residence and scrambling for benefices on the part of many of the senior fellows. Comparatively few of them seem to have been actively engaged in college teaching. William

Ludlam was exceptional in that, not being a tutor, he lectured conscientiously in mathematics from 1746 to 1769, doubtless at the expense of the pastoral duties he owed to his Leicestershire livings. In general, however, college lectureships were declining into sinecures during this period. John Gibson (B.A. 1671) attended morning philosophy lectures in the hall and Ambrose Bonwicke in 1710 kept at least three logic and one Greek lectures each week. In 1738, however, order was given that the 'two logic tables be joined', suggesting that, where two lecturers had been engaged, there would now be only one; and in 1764, although there was a Hebrew lecturer in the person of Israel Lyons, he was no longer one of the fellows. In fact, the provisions of the statutes in regard to college instruction, as in regard to other things, were coming to be more honoured in the breach than in the observance. It grievously concerned Ambrose Bonwicke that 'the governing part of the whole college should annul a law by their practice'.[1]

Yet where laws fell into desuetude the customs of the college came to fill the gap. Instruction was coming to be mainly a tutorial responsibility even in Richard Holdsworth's day; and in 1668 John Gibson once or twice a week read at night in his tutor's chambers Homer or the Greek Testament. By the time Ambrose Bonwicke came up in 1710 tutorial lecturing was obviously important, for he refers more than once, not only to the 'exercises of the house', but to his tutor's private lectures.[2] While tutors engrossed educational responsibility, they also became fewer. Soon after the Restoration tutorial duties ceased to be incumbent upon all fellows. During the later seventeenth century they were discharged mainly by three men: Thomas Watson (1660–79), Francis Roper (1666–81) and Arthur Orchard (1666–1702); and in the eighteenth century the college settled down into two 'sides' in the charge of such men as Thomas Rutherford, described by Cole as a 'chief pupil-monger' at St John's. Rutherford became regius professor of divinity in 1756 and conformed to the custom of that chair by never lecturing; but as tutor he had lectured, for he published the substance of his courses on mathematics and on Grotius's *De Jure Belli et Pacis*.

At the same time, busy chief pupil-mongers were unable, and might be unwilling, to meet all the needs of their pupils for instruction. Thomas Frampton was a tutor 1764–71, a man whom Cole describes as 'rather fat, a great sporter and much of a gentleman...[who] married a Mrs Arbuthnot's daughter, who kept the Hoop tavern'; but he was also 'fonder of sporting and Newmarket than of books and his college'. The office of lecturing his pupils devolved upon his assistants, Richard Raikes and William Pearce, young men but recently elected to fellowships.[1] The habit of tutors to appoint sub-tutors to perform lecturing work was already of some antiquity. Thomas Balguy, three years after he was elected a fellow in 1741, was appointed assistant tutor by William Powell and his lecture notes on moral philosophy and on the evidences of natural and revealed religion are preserved in the college library.[2] Earlier still, the sub-tutor who lectured Ambrose Bonwicke on mathematics was John Newcome, later full tutor and master. He had already served as *lector matutinus* (1707), sub-lecturer in hall (1708), examiner in philosophy (1709), lecturer in cosmography, examiner in rhetoric (1710) and lecturer in geometry (1711).[3] His rapid progress through these somewhat diverse offices suggests that probably they entailed small duties; and that sub-tutorial lecturing by young fellows employed by one or other of the two chief tutors, together with such lecturing as the chief tutors themselves felt called upon to do, had more or less supplanted the statutory provision for the instruction of undergraduates.

By contrast with earlier days, then, teaching and a responsibility for undergraduates had ceased to be a matter for all fellows. There were only two principal pupil-mongers occupying the office of tutor, standing *in loco parentis* to their respective sides, engaging assistants who helped them to teach their pupils, and collecting the fees which undergraduates owed for tuition and maintenance.[4] Tutors and assistant-tutors, however, were only a part of the fellowship. Of the rest, some were incumbents of other college offices—were deans, bursars and so forth; some were more or less non-resident; and a few might mainly devote themselves to scholarship. Among this last group, we have a pleasant glimpse of 'Demosthenes

Taylor'. 'If you called on him in college after dinner, you were sure to find him at an oval walnut-tree table', which (like the floor) was 'entirely covered with books'. The intrusion was not resented, for he would call at once for pipes and glasses and fall 'to procuring a small place for the bottle just to stand on'. If Taylor prevents us from forgetting that the college might be a place of learning, there were others among the fellows who fit all too well the conventional caricature of the eighteenth-century don. Samuel Ogden, for example, was elected a fellow in 1740 and spent the years 1744–53 as master of Heath Grammar School, Halifax, holding also two curacies in that neighbourhood. He then returned into residence, occupied various college offices and was eventually president from 1763 to 1767. He was also vicar of a Wiltshire parish from 1744 to 1766, vicar of the Round Church in Cambridge from 1758, rector of Stansfield in Suffolk from 1766 and of Lawford in Essex from 1767, all until his death.

This manifold preferment by no means assuaged Ogden's appetite. He considered becoming a candidate for the chair of Arabic, he was a candidate for the mastership in 1765 and 1775 and he did obtain the Woodwardian chair of geology in 1764. This last appointment has been called a scandalous one, and to say the least it had a certain strangeness. Ogden's most obvious qualification was that he fulfilled the statutory requirement that the occupant of the Woodwardian chair must be unmarried. Any others that he might have had he did not test too seriously, following professorial custom in that day by refraining from lecturing even though he did, apparently, display some interest in the arrangement of the geological specimens in his custody as professor. It was even said that the manner in which he came by his chair was not entirely respectable. It was still in the gift of the last surviving executor of John Woodward, who was then 'dying and in indifferent circumstances', and moreover possessed of a daughter he wished to dower and marry. Ogden's gift of £200 for that purpose, rumour had it, secured his succession. None the less, and for all his 'uncivilized appearance' (Newcastle, we are told, found that 'the doctor was not a producible man'), Ogden could be good company. Cole found him a 'great epicure' who loved 'a cheerful glass, at ease in his armchair, nightcap, nightgown

58

IV. SAMUEL OGDEN, PRESIDENT 1763–1767

and slippers, and no ladies present'. His end had its appropriateness, for it was occasioned 'by eating too late at night a larger supper on bread and cheese and ale than usual'.

IV

From fellows we must turn to undergraduates. Their numbers, as we have seen, were falling and they were somewhat older when they came up than formerly, though even in the 1720's Heberden and Rutherford both entered when they were fourteen. On the other hand, the catchment area continued to expand. In the century beginning in 1665 there were three entrants from France (perhaps Huguenot refugees), one from Holland, thirty-four from Ireland and (after 1715) five from Scotland. As notable was the growing trickle from the New World, the sons of planters, lawyers, government servants and soldiers: five are described simply as of American origin, five came from mainland America, thirteen from Barbados, six from Jamaica and two each from Montserrat and St Christopher. At home, school connections remained important. Throughout the period Sedbergh was by far the largest provider, but by the eighteenth century Eton had moved up into second place.

Given the character of the evidence, it is a good deal more difficult to establish at all clearly the backgrounds of undergraduates. It would seem, however, that relatively few of them were sons of mercantile families at any time during this period; and that in general, so far as the social composition of the college is concerned, there was little to distinguish the second half of the seventeenth century from the 1630's. Sons of noblemen and gentlemen were not quite so numerous; sons of professional men, especially of clergymen, were somewhat more numerous; and sons of artisan and farming families still constituted nearly a third of the college. The years after 1715, however, saw some changes of emphasis. Sons of professional men (of the clergy especially, but also of doctors, lawyers and men in the public service in increasing numbers) came to be about two fifths of the body of undergraduates. Sons of noblemen and gentlemen, 41 per cent of the entry in the years 1630–65, declined to about 28 per cent; and boys from relatively poorer families, especially from the poorer country families, declined from about a third to about a quarter of those coming up. It may also be significant in this connection that the number of sizars admitted also began to fall after 1680 and with some rapidity after 1740, averaging thirteen each year in the 1760's compared with thirty-three or thirty-four in the decade or two after the Restoration. Certainly fewer men were coming up altogether in the eighteenth century, but the proportion of them who were sizars also fell. In the 1660's it was more than half; in the 1760's it was a good deal less than half.

The interpretation of these statistics, imperfect as they are in themselves, is far from easy. Perhaps it ought first to be said that the fall by about half in the size of the college was below the average for the time; for between 1620 and 1760 the number of men matriculating each year at Cambridge fell by some two thirds. On the other hand, the college's losses appear to have been in some degree selective. It no longer attracted in the eighteenth century quite so many gentlemen's sons and its doors were not quite so open as they had been to boys from poorer homes. It was, in consequence, training somewhat fewer of the governors of the English counties and the English kingdom, though it trained more of those who would play a part in colonial territories. It also contributed less to that social mobility which had been so remarkable a feature of Tudor and Stuart England. It became, in fact, more markedly a means by which the professional classes (and for the time being most particularly the clergy) perpetuated their hold upon their professions. These impressions are endorsed by what we know of the subsequent careers of the men who passed through the college in the decade beginning in 1715. Only about 13 per cent of them went out into the world as gentlemen or peers, and only 6 per cent as members of the legal and medical professions. Four fifths, on the other hand, became clergymen, sometimes doubling clerical preferment with college fellowships or masterships of schools. The church absorbed every sort of man who came to the college. Many who became clergymen were themselves sons of clergymen. The attainment of a benefice by way of the university was still the most obvious way for a poor man's son to rise in the world; but more than half of the gentlemen's sons in the college were likewise destined for a clerical career. Many of them, doubtless, were younger sons deprived of expectations from their family estates by the régime of strict settlements.[1]

In terms of output, then, the college was, at least as much as ever it had been, a school of theology. How adequately did its educational provision match this function? Fellows continued to be under an obligation to proceed to the B.D. degree; but, as we have seen, not all were resident and divinity professors did not very often provide lectures for their instruction. Thus, even the possession of a divinity degree can hardly presuppose, of necessity, systematic and profound study in theology. Fellows, in any case, were a small minority of those who passed through the college. The majority, if they took any degree at all, went down as soon as they had proceeded B.A. The undergraduate courses taken by John Gibson, Abraham de la Pryme and Ambrose Bonwicke, who came up respectively in 1667, 1694 and 1710, were basically philosophical in character. The last two, however, found physics and mathematics bulking larger and the emphasis on mathematics continued to increase.[2] In the first half of the eighteenth century the traditional disputations by which men were tested for their degrees began to give way to a new public examination, at first oral and later written, to determine fitness for the B.A. degree. At the same time, as Thomas Gray lamented in 1736, the classics fell into great contempt and the content of the public examination came to be overwhelmingly mathematical. Finally, in 1763, the sheep submitting themselves to this examination were separated from the goats. Candidates were grouped according to ability, and mathematical ability at that. Only the better men were examined for an honours degree and the rest were less strenuously tested for a degree without honours.[3]

The effect of these changes can be put quite simply. Only about ten Johnians a year between 1748 and 1760 proceeded B.A. with honours; and perhaps even their mathematical expertness ought not to be set too high. A generation later, Henry Gunning's examination experiences might seem less harrowing to the modern mathematician than they did to him: 'the first and second problems were for the extraction of the square and cube roots, and what was never before heard of, everyone *was required to attempt them as far as three places of decimals*' (the italics are his).[1] On the other hand, two out of three undergraduates did not aim so high as this. Either they did not graduate at all, or they did so without honours on the results of an examination which made less strenuous demands upon them. The fact that, in the 1750's, about one in every six undergraduates was a fellow commoner, often not inclined or even expected to take academic studies too seriously, must have contributed to this situation; but so did the fact that Cambridge's mathematical bias was clean out of line with the classical bent of school curricula, and the fact that not all men are mathematically inclined. Even so serious, indeed priggish, a lad as Ambrose Bonwicke had to admit that he found the subject difficult.[2] Its relevance, too, may not always have appeared self-evident to would-be clergymen, the average undergraduates in the college. It was the utility of the study which was questioned by John Mainwaring, senior bursar of St John's for nearly twenty years and Zachary Brooke's successor in the Lady Margaret chair. He was prepared to admit that, in the hands of a master, mathematics 'may be the means of furthering discoveries in natural philosophy'; but in general he wished 'to bring back our studies to the plain old road of nature and common sense' and 'to establish merit on a *broader* as well as on a *sounder* basis'. His specific might have its own defects, but it is hard not to feel that he had discerned a genuine failing in the Cambridge education of that day.[3]

The deficiencies in the system, combined with the presence in the college of some men without much inclination or intent to study, might well make for idleness and those other faults for which the eighteenth-century undergraduate has a certain notoriety. At least there was sometimes rowdiness enough to incommode those of more sober disposition. Christopher Hull, in a letter to his father in 1762 which gives no favourable impression of his literacy, had to report how he had been 'rioted' in his rooms and how he had laid in a stout poker as a weapon of defence.[4] On the other hand, the number of those who frittered away their time, even the number of fellow commoners who did so, ought not to be exaggerated out of all proportion. There would be nothing inappropriate in the supposition that Robert Smith (B.A. 1720) and Samuel Pegge (B.A. 1726) first began to develop their antiquarian interests in the college of Thomas Baker; and it is likely enough that Soame Jenyns, though he took no degree, was already cultivating those literary tastes which made him in his day a popular author. In some cases, indeed, we can be quite sure that what was officially required of undergraduates left room for the profitable pursuit of private interests. Ambrose Bonwicke was able to find time for devotional reading, to learn French under a private tutor and translate Boileau; and Abraham de la Pryme was not prevented from indulging his taste for natural history, chemistry and magic.[1] To this extent, the prescribed curriculum for degrees, and even its increasingly mathematical character, did not positively preclude the college from offering the opportunity for a liberal education.

In general, however, the total impression we get of the unreformed college is not one of intense intellectual life. Not too much was asked of those who wished to enter it: as Abraham de la Pryme tells us, 'I was examined by my tutor, then by the senior dean, and then by the junior dean and then by the master, who all made me but construe a verse or two apiece in the Greek Testament, except the master, who asked me both in that and in Plautus and Horace too'. Scholars, it is true, were more thoroughly tested: a regular scholarship examination was envisaged by a college order of 1678 and twenty years earlier John Gibson was examined in Aristotle, Homer, logic and the Greek Testament.[2] Those who went for honours, too, were strictly if narrowly examined as things went in those times. Yet some of the earnestness seems to have gone out of the life of the college, perhaps in part because the religious passions of an earlier generation had cooled. At the same time, the increasingly mathematical orientation of studies, and the long tail of men who did not aim at honours or even at any degree at all, would seem to have contributed to the same end. To that extent the college had less to give to English life than it had under the Tudors and the early Stuarts. It could still produce a Matthew Prior, a Heberden, a Ludlam; but the St John's of Samuel Ogden was, on the whole, a college needing a measure of reform.

IV

THE AGE OF REFORM
(1765-1882)

It is, in the nature of things, impossible to fasten upon a precise date on one side of which lies unreformed Cambridge and on the other the age of reform. Reform was inevitably intermittent; it could be halted or qualified by defenders of old ways or of vested interests; and it required time to produce its harvest of results. The most recent historian of the university has chosen the year 1800, as a date of convenience, for his watershed.[1] It is a point in time as good as any other for the purpose; and yet, if we fix our eyes only upon St John's College, there is also something to be said for regarding the mastership of William Samuel Powell (1765-75) as the beginning of a new age. It is true that, until William Henry Bateson became master in 1857, St John's was more likely to be found in the rear-guard than in the van of reform. On the other hand, between Powell's day and Bateson's, there was also some consistency in the attempt to introduce a measure of improvement into the ways in which the college fulfilled its duty and purpose. In that sense there was a real, if tenuous, continuity between Powell's new broom in 1765 and the sweeping reforms of the third quarter of the nineteenth century, the period which, without too much exaggeration, may be called the age of Bateson.

I

The way in which Powell became master hardly seemed to presage re-forming tendencies: on the contrary, it looked like the high-water mark of college politics in the eighteenth-century manner, with Newcastle as usual pulling the strings. The first moves were played in 1758 when news came that Newcome was ill ('his disorder is the hickups'). The main contenders for the succession were Powell, Rutherford and the inevitable Zachary Brooke. Powell, as a Tory and a client of the Townshends, had to Newcastle's mind to be kept out at any cost: it was hoped, therefore, that Rutherford, perhaps because he was unswervingly loyal to Newcastle, could be persuaded to retire from the contest, thus enabling the anti-Powell voters to plump for Brooke. The latter never came so near being master again, for in the event Newcome recovered and Powell learned his lesson. He transferred his allegiance to Newcastle just at the moment when Brooke defected from that camp. The result was that, when New-come did die in 1765, Newcastle decided again to sacrifice Rutherford and to back Powell, who seemed to have more support among the fellows. On the other hand, it was by no means clear that his support was enough and there were rivals other than Rutherford: Ogden, hovering on the fringes of the contest, and Brooke at first until he decided to withdraw in favour of that popular and sporting tutor, Thomas Frampton. Deadlock seemed neatly to have been achieved.

It was broken by an approach from a somewhat oblique angle. Dr Newcome's death vacated the Lady Margaret chair as well as the master-ship, and to fill that chair required the suffrages of resident doctors and bachelors of divinity. Owing to the fact that nearly all fellows of St John's were under statutory obligation to proceed B.D. and that its fellowship was large, the college was apt to have the preponderant voice in choosing the Lady Margaret professor, particularly since college loyalties weighed more than any pretence of assessing the respective merits of rival candidates. The outcome was, indeed, that every Lady Margaret professor from 1688 to 1875 was either a master or a fellow of the college. The situation did not go unperceived by Newcastle, for only a year before he had observed that 'you gentlemen of St John's, having so many bachelors of divinity, look upon yourself as having a right to that professorship'. He now proceeded to turn it to account. Powell supported Brooke for the Lady Margaret chair; Brooke persuaded Frampton to withdraw from the contest for the mastership and to cast his influence on Powell's side; and Powell's election became a foregone conclusion. Dr Ogden, however, had the last word: 'the Lady Margaret,...as I apprehend, has made the master'.[1]

Yet for all this exercise in eighteenth-century political intrigue, Powell was soon at work upon improvements. He had scarcely been installed when an order went out for twice-yearly college examinations for all undergraduates. The syllabus was not, perhaps, excessively stringent. In 1783, first-year men were examined in Horace's *Epistles*, Tacitus's *Agricola*, some algebra and Euclid, elementary logic and Beausobre's *Introduction to the Reading of the Holy Scriptures*; and, generally speaking, men of each year were tested in a modicum of mathematics and logic, one or two classical texts, and perhaps Butler's *Analogy* or the first book of Locke's *Human Understanding*.[2] College examinations did mean, however, that progress was regularly assessed and, while those who did badly were punished or censured, those who did well were rewarded by prizes and proper encouragement. Powell himself closely supervised the conduct of these examinations, tightened the procedure for examining for scholarships, and followed the example Richard Bentley had set at Trinity by erecting an observatory on the Shrewsbury tower in second court. William Ludlam was soon using it to make astronomical observations, which he published in a substantial volume in 1769. In the course of his work he made use of the clock which still tells the time in the college library and established the fact that it 'has been more regular than that at Greenwich'.[3]

Powell was no less concerned for the moral and religious training of the 'young scholars' of the college. He set an example by never failing to appear for 6 a.m. chapel, instituted an annual examination in one of the Gospels or the Acts, and saw that the choir was kept up to strength with singing men and singing boys.[4] All in all, his policy notably enhanced the college's reputation. An observer found there in 1775 'each valuable Greek and Roman author with ardour studied; each source of sound philosophy with zeal explored;...a numerous set of learned persons improving youth of the most respectable families...in every branch of useful literature'.[5]

The encomium may exaggerate, but an improved reputation at least reversed the trend for the size of the college to decrease. The low average of thirty-one admissions yearly in the 1750's was raised to one of forty-six in the 1770's. Nor did academic reform exhaust Powell's endeavours, for he also improved the college's business organization. He introduced a new form of accounts in 1770 designed to give a comprehensive view of income and expenditure—an indispensable step if some old abuses were to be weeded out and if any well-grounded financial policy was to be framed. He was also much concerned with the college's buildings and grounds. In 1772–6, under the superintendence of James Essex, the south range of first court was refaced with ashlar, the windows were sashed and the building was raised to convert the garrets into a full storey. At the same time, the internal arrangement of the chambers was modified in order to turn this range, like the southern range of third court, into one of 'double-banked' rooms; and this change in turn made necessary the insertion of the central chimney stacks. If these operations were the first attack on the architectural homogeneity of first court, Powell was happier in his dealings with the Backs. There the Wilderness was laid out by 'Capability' Brown, converting it in all probability from an older formal garden into the 'natural' garden we know today.[1] The cost of these various enterprises was met in part by an appeal to old members of the college, to which Powell himself contributed £500.

If Powell and the Johnians were reformers within the college, they were less enthusiastic for reforms outside it. A move to abolish the rule of celibacy, and to allow a man to have 'a wife and a fellowship with her', is said to have aroused some enthusiasm in the college in 1766, but there is nothing to show that Powell shared it. On two other questions his attitude is abundantly clear. When an attempt was made in 1771 to modify the obligation of B.A.'s to subscribe to the Thirty-nine Articles of the Church of England, he was among 'the first who placed themselves in the gap against these innovations'; and in like manner he led the opposition to a proposal for instituting regular university examinations on the model of the college examinations he had established in St John's. He saw no need for such a step, for other colleges could follow the Johnian example; and great danger in it, since 'the business of education…is conducted with more success…under the domestic discipline of each college'.[1] Collegiate autonomy, in short, must not be prejudiced by enlarging the university's responsibility. Here, as in his illiberality to nonconformity, Powell was clean opposed to principles which would prevail in the nineteenth century. It was not for nothing that he had been brought up in the college pre-eminent in Cambridge for its Anglicanism and Toryism.

Eighteenth-century ways of making masters were still not quite un-thinkable in 1775 when Powell died. Great patrons arrayed themselves for the contest. The archbishop of Canterbury and other prelates, with Lord North and other peers, intervened on behalf of Dr Beadon. Samuel Ogden made positively his last appearance, withdrawing when he found he could count only upon three votes. In the end, however, John Chevallier was elected, supported mainly by 'the junior part of the college', by a majority of a single vote. Ill-health and a good-natured disposition made him a far less dominating ruler than Powell.[2] He was succeeded in 1789 by William Craven, a scholar who had been fourth wrangler, chancellor's medallist and professor of Arabic, and who composed notes for a syllabus of universal history. Craven's mastership, however, exactly spanned the French Revolutionary and Napoleonic eras, when Isaac Milner's determi-nation to 'have nothing to do with Jacobins and infidels' held the field in Cambridge and could be stretched to cover almost any suggestion for change. The years 1775–1815, therefore, lacked the dynamic character of Powell's decade. Efforts to encourage academic effort and to insist upon firm discipline continued; a rat catcher was employed in 1795; and Craven instituted Sunday lectures on the Gospels and the Acts, if only to keep Johnians away from Charles Simeon's evangelical sermons. These were small beer after Powell's pyrotechnics, and it ought to be added that Craven did not prevent Simeon from making converts. Most notable among them was Henry Martyn, senior wrangler in 1801 and fellow in 1802. His evangelical faith took him, in 1805, to labour as a missionary in the east for the few years of life which remained to him. The memorial of those years, spent in preaching the Gospel in India and Persia, were translations of the Prayer Book and New Testament into Hindustani and of the latter also into Persian.[1]

The slowing down of change after 1775 affords an opportunity to assess the total impact of Powell's reforms. His efforts to impose a more conscientious discharge of their duties upon college officers were not altogether successful. William Wood, senior bursar 1795–8, still speculated with college money, a fact which came to light when relatives with whom he had placed it failed during a bank crisis; and there was also some difficulty in persuading college examiners to fulfil their office.[2] More important, even Powell's educational reforms did not effect a complete regeneration. He had tried to insist that fellow commoners should submit to the same requirements as others, but their spirits were not always willing nor did tutors always co-operate. Castlereagh confessed to no enthusiasm for being 'immured in Cambridge and plodding for fame'; and William Wilberforce, although he did well in classics, neglected mathematics and 'was told I was too clever to require them'. The continued primacy of mathematics in the honours course, moreover, was still a deterrent to some. George Tennyson, the poet laureate's father, considered that to excel in this subject 'would require such continual application and exertion as would neither suit my health, time nor inclination. The anxiety I should suffer and the deprivation of better knowledge could only be compensated by the hope of an uncertain and at best a transitory honour.'

The Cambridge career of William Wordsworth, however, throws as clear a light as any other upon the scope and limitations of educational opportunities at St John's at this time. He came up in 1787 from Hawkshead school, which had good connections with St John's (still 'a haven of north countrymen') and good enough teaching to give Wordsworth a year's start over most other freshmen. This advantage, as he confessed in later years, was unlucky for him. He made a good beginning as this was measured by college examinations and was soon elected a scholar, but drifted thereafter into those easy-going ways he described in the *Prelude*:

> Companionships,
> Friendships, acquaintances, were welcome all.
> We sauntered, played or rioted; we talked
> Unprofitable talk at morning hours;
> Drifted along the streets and walks,
> Read lazily in trivial books, went forth
> To gallop through the country in blind zeal
> Of senseless horsemanship, or on the breast
> Of Cam sailed boisterously.

A first reaction to these lines might be that there is a good deal that never changes in the undergraduate life of all times, that there may be profit to be drawn from unprofitable talk and lessons to be learned from trivial books. On the other hand, it is true that Wordsworth, like Castlereagh, was disinclined towards plodding for fame as St John's College measured it. He 'refused to do the necessary mathematics' and put himself out of court for honours. Yet he also enjoyed what Leslie Stephen called 'the advantages to be derived from the neglect of his teachers', pursuing his own interests in the literature of the ancient world and of the Europe of his day.[1]

It may be negative commendation to say that the college did not prevent Wordsworth from pursuing a course of self-education and of the education to be got from friendships, companionships and acquaintanceships. It must also be admitted that his proceedings did not conform to Powell's expectations of a young scholar. Yet the fact that he did get his own sort of education is merely one of the curious and contradictory features about the college's history at this time. Another is the fact that St John's, for all its conservatism, bred some notable reformers. It was the college of Robert Clarkson, son of a Wisbech schoolmaster, and of William Wilberforce, a Hull merchant's son, who worked together with such effect for the abolition of the slave trade. It was also the college of two notable Londoners: of Samuel Whitbread, likewise a supporter of negro emancipation and of reform in general; and of John Horne Tooke, who crusaded for Wilkes and liberty and still dared to be a radical in the far more difficult days of the 1790's, when fear of the French Revolution had made radicalism treason.

Turning from individuals to the whole body of the college, it must first be said that, partly because of the wars, the recovery of numbers under Powell was not quite maintained under his successors. Once again, moreover, we must point to the limited success of his educational reforms. Of 385 men who came up in the 1790's,[1] leaving aside those who died before graduating and one who eloped with an Ely girl to Gretna Green, nearly a third took no degree at all. One undergraduate in twenty was the son of a nobleman and eligible for the M.A. degree without examination; and a few others took the LL.B. or M.B. degrees. Less than two thirds, therefore, took the B.A. degree and only about one fifth of all undergraduates had skill enough in mathematics to do so with honours. The rest, like George Tennyson or William Wordsworth, were 'poll men' (a description derived from οἱ πολλοί, indicating the modest intellectual distinction which was absolutely required of them). The picture, indeed, is slightly worse rather than better when we compare it with the 1750's. The fault lay partly in the system, with its mathematical bias; but it is also clear that the college was generous to mediocrity and small endeavour.

A closer study of this same generation of undergraduates suggests that other changes had taken place. Sons of mercantile and banking families were neither more nor less numerous than in the past, but more undergraduates were sons of gentlemen and substantially more were sons of peers than had been the case earlier in the eighteenth century. Professional families hold their own with a notable exception: sons of the clergy fell by almost a half. Sons of artisans and small farmers, too, seem virtually to have disappeared. It is true that the admission register is often defective in the information it gives about parental status, so that when it tells us nothing we may have upon our hands men drawn from these classes or from the families of poorer clergymen. There is still a strong suggestion, however, that the range of recruitment, viewed from the social angle, was narrower than in the past. This implication finds some support in the fact that, in the 1790's, only half as many sizars were admitted as in the 1750's and that, in the 1750's, only half as many had been admitted as at the beginning of the century. Perhaps, too, this is the gloss we should put upon the information that, under Powell, the college was engaged in 'improving youth of the most respectable families'; and one consequence may have been some slight decline in the proportion of undergraduates at St John's engaged in honours courses.

If from this point of view the college community was becoming less varied, there is another respect in which the reverse is true. Just over half the undergraduates of the 1790's made their careers in the church, a sharp drop from the figure of four fifths at the beginning of the century. Conversely, the college trained more peers, more gentry and more West Indian planters, simply because more of its undergraduates came from these classes. It produced fewer doctors (not surprisingly in view of the low reputation of the Cambridge medical school). On the other hand, it turned out four times as many lawyers, and more men who went into the armed forces (this due in part to the wars) and into the government and colonial services. The ultimate purposes which were being served by the college as a place of education were once again becoming more diverse.

11

After William Craven died in the year of Waterloo the pressures making for change became stronger. An unprecedented economic transformation affected the position of the college as a landowning corporation, diversified still further the demands which society made upon it, enlarged the opportunities open to those who passed through the college and created new classes of men who sought a university education for their sons. These forces, in combination with the steady growth of population, made for rising numbers. In the 1790's there were only about 120 men in residence and just over forty coming up each year. In 1851 the annual entry was ninety and there were 371 in residence; and in 1880 the entry had risen still further to 104.[1] Expansion at this rate made new demands upon the college's resources, accommodation and educational organization.

The political climate was also changing. The Anglican monopoly of English public life, which the Restoration of Charles II had made definitive, was questioned, modified and in the end in great measure overthrown.

This was a matter which profoundly affected colleges, clerical communities which reflected the Anglican dominion in its purest form. It was achieved mainly through the action of the state: one manifestation of a general increase in government regulation of colleges and universities, not as an exercise of patronage as in the times of the Stuarts or old Newcastle, but as part of the new régime of Benthamite social engineering. It was a trend, moreover, which did more than make colleges increasingly susceptible to the play of public authority. The result, in the end, reversed the whole tendency which, since the sixteenth century, had made colleges virtually autonomous and the university, as such, of small account in the work of education at Cambridge.

James Wood, however, who succeeded Craven as master in 1815, was in most ways typical of an older world. The son of a Lancashire weaver, he was enabled to come to St John's by the award of a sizarship (showing that, if such opportunities were rather fewer in the later eighteenth century, they had not disappeared). As an undergraduate he kept in a garret called the Tub at the top of O staircase, second court, and read by a candle on the stairs with his feet in straw, being too poor to afford a light or fire. He was fully in tune with the mathematical emphasis in the curriculum of the time, for he was senior wrangler in 1782 and the author of mathematical treatises which served as university text-books for thirty or forty years.[1] In the old manner he combined his mastership with other preferment, becoming dean of Ely in 1820 and rector of the college living of Freshwater in the Isle of Wight in 1823. In other ways, too, he was conservative. In 1817, as vice-chancellor, he suppressed the Union Society for presuming to debate political questions and he was a natural confidant for Dr Butler, headmaster of Shrewsbury, who thought the Union did 'fatal mischief' to men of first-rate talents.[2] Wood's churchmanship was also conventional. He was 'firmly attached to...decent ceremonial and moderate discipline, both as distinguished from bigotry and enthusiasm'. From this sprang his care for the chapel: a new organ, with three manuals and pedals probably for the first time, was built in 1839; the college combined with Trinity to set up a joint choir school for their singing boys; chapel reading prizes were established; and Wood left £20,000 to the college to provide the nucleus of a fund for building a new chapel.

This benefaction was half only of Wood's residuary estate and had been preceded by gifts of almost equal amount during his lifetime. The scale of his generosity is at first sight surprising when the poverty of his beginnings is remembered; but it is some indication of the rewards to be got from a plurality of college offices and benefices in the church. To that extent a sizarship might still be an avenue to affluence. At the same time, Wood's benefactions are testimony to his real and enduring concern for the college he served for fifty-seven years. He became a fellow in 1782, was soon made an assistant tutor and was a full tutor from 1789 to 1814, serving also as president from 1802 until he became master. The college had much opportunity, therefore, to assess his fitness to govern it and the qualities he had already displayed before he became master were succinctly summarized by one of the fellows: 'his sound and cautious understanding, seconded by unremitting diligence, by remarkable punctuality and rigid adherence to *order* in all his arrangements, particularly qualified him for the able discharge of the practical duties of life.'[1]

Sound administration and cautious improvement were to be expected, therefore, under Wood's rule, but no welcoming enthusiasm for drastic innovation in the church or the university or in public affairs. There is evidence enough of his attitude and the college's in the latter respect. Palmerston tells us that, in 1826, only the loyalty of Johnians to him as a member of the college allayed their 'violent language' against Catholic emancipation; and the college in 1833 once more stoutly opposed a move to abolish subscription to the Thirty-nine Articles. One result of its success in this last endeavour was that John Joseph Sylvester, second wrangler in 1837, could not graduate because he was a Jew. He did not, in fact, proceed B.A. until 1872, after the abolition of religious tests, and it was only in 1880 that the college elected him an honorary fellow.[2] Meantime, the subscription controversy had grown into something more ominous. In 1837 the earl of Radnor moved the appointment of a commission to enquire into the statutes and administration of colleges.

St John's was strong for a petition against this interference, although Wood saw the expediency of concerting with the visitor such alterations in its statutes 'as may quiet the public mind, which is at present a little excited against us'. In the event, the earl of Radnor's bill failed and it was possible to postpone the disagreeable task of altering the statutes.[1]

In 1837, however, the college had been able to inform the vice-chancellor that a commission was unnecessary because it possessed and had already exercised powers of amending its statutes.[2] The claim was just and the modification had been substantial. The Elizabethan statutes, which were still in force, prevented the college from having at any one time more than two fellows born in any given English county or more than one from certain Welsh dioceses. The disadvantages of this rule had long been clear.[3] It had compelled Richard Bentley, at the end of the seventeenth century, to migrate to Trinity because the Yorkshire fellowships at St John's were full. Bentley's stormy career as master of his adopted college may have left some doubt as to where the best of that bargain lay; but there could be less argument about the benefit derived by Trinity from the migration of Thomas Jones, when he saw no chance of obtaining the only fellowship at St John's open to those born in the diocese of St Asaph. He proved a successful mathematical teacher and was senior tutor for the twenty years after 1787. In that office 'he raised the reputation and thereby increased the numbers of Trinity, so that at the opening of the new century it had fairly taken the lead in the Cambridge world', surpassing for the first time (at least in size) the college which Thomas Jones had left to go there.[4]

This growth of Trinity provoked much rivalry between it and St John's, and this may have been one of the reasons which moved Wood to seek an amendment of the fellowship statute. The statutes, by this time, had been unchanged for so long that there was dubiety even about the procedure for altering them. The lawyers, too, did not encourage the master, but Wood enlisted the aid of a Johnian M.P., J. C. Villiers, and won the benevolence of Sidmouth, the Home Secretary. In 1819 the college formally presented a petition asking that it might award the thirty-two foundress's fellowships without restriction as to place of birth, leaving untouched the qualifications attached to the twenty-one fellowships founded by private benefactors. The petition was granted and it was further provided that a foundress's fellow, if qualified, might be removed to a private foundation without loss of seniority, thus freeing a fellowship which could be filled without restriction. In this way the college sought to ensure that 'the very best scholars and the most deserving young men' would not be kept out of fellowships by mere accident of birthplace and, at the same time, that there might be better candidates available for privately endowed fellowships than there had been for the Keton fellowship in 1775: William Wood, who had been 'wooden spoon' (that is, last in the third class) of the mathematical honours list, and C. W. Abson who had graduated without honours at all.[1]

James Wood, in this particular, served the college well and he did so, too, in providing it with new buildings. These enabled a great part of the increased numbers coming up after the Napoleonic wars to be accommodated in college without sacrificing the practice, which became the rule in the eighteenth century, for each man to have a set to himself (Henry Kirke White, the poet, speaks in 1805 of his 'three rooms: a sitting room, a bedroom and a kind of scullery or pantry'). The decision to build was taken in 1824 and in the following year it was agreed that the site should be across the river from third court. The work had been done by 1831 after Rickman and Hutchinson's design, creating 'the largest single building until then put up by any college'. It was linked to the older courts by the so-called 'Bridge of Sighs' which Queen Victoria thought 'so pretty and picturesque'; and, in Dr Pevsner's judgement, the new court's 'fairy sky-line...looks very well as a backcloth to the landscaped grounds from Trinity northward'.[2] Whatever judgement we pass upon its aesthetic appeal, there is no question that it was costly. The bill was £78,000. With only £9000 in the college's building fund, £65,000 had to be borrowed; and, though Wood gave handsomely and other donors contributed £5000, the debt was not cleared until 1857. By that time £41,000 had been paid in interest charges, a heavy increment to the initial cost.[3] To this charge, moreover, had to be added more modest expenditure incurred in completing and laying out the Backs more or less in their present form. When St Giles's parish was enclosed in 1805, two small areas adjoining the fellows' garden and a larger plot to the north of it, later an orchard, were acquired. They were absorbed into the landscaped grounds in 1822–4, the 'Broad Walk' leading to Queens' Road was laid down on its present line, and the existing gateway was erected and closed with a gate which came, apparently, from Horseheath Hall. Before building began upon the new court its backcloth had been prepared.[1]

In Wood's last years and for a time after Ralph Tatham succeeded him in 1839, there was again something of a pause in the operations of change. This interlude invites a glance at the college as it was on the eve of the great reforms which took place in the third quarter of the nineteenth century. The mathematical bias of undergraduate studies still persisted, but with some modification. The classical tripos had come into existence in 1824, though candidates for classical honours had still first to obtain mathematical honours. A broadening of the mathematical curriculum, moreover, made this hurdle somewhat stiffer. A high proportion of undergraduates, therefore, remained satisfied with the ordinary degree. One 'undergraduate of no importance' tells us: 'I never really like mathematics ...I was content to go for a pass in the poll'; while a contemporary observed in retrospect: 'if there had been a moral sciences or an historical or a law tripos in my day, I might have quitted the college with greater credit than I did'. The pace for poll men, moreover, had not become more strenuous. One, at least, attended as few classical and mathematical lectures as possible, 'having soon discovered I knew enough to pass for the ordinary degree'.[2]

St John's was conservative in its honours men, as it was in other respects. To an American in Cambridge it was at once the 'hot bed of bigotry' and the 'nursery of senior wranglers',[3] for about twenty-nine men took the mathematical tripos each year as against eight who took classics. On the other hand, academic standards were rising somewhat. About one third of Johnian undergraduates now went for honours and the college's mathematical reputation probably helped to attract to it such men as John

Frederick William Herschel (B.A. 1813), Sylvester and John Couch Adams (B.A. 1843). It was, however, something more than merely a mathematical academy. John Stevens Henslow (B.A. 1818), professor first of mineralogy and then of botany, was one who broke the bad old tradition that professors did not lecture, and he did work which influenced Darwin as well as securing for the latter his passage on the *Beagle*; W. H. Miller (B.A. 1826), who became professor of mineralogy in 1832, placed the science of crystallography on a sound mathematical basis; and John Haviland (B.A. 1807) was largely responsible for reforms in the medical curriculum which made the later history of the Cambridge medical school 'a monument to his saving grace'. Charles Cardale Babington (B.A. 1830), likewise, displayed a variety of talents, for he was at once a field botanist, an archaeologist and an entomologist (hence the nickname 'Beetles Babington'); and these talents he exercised over a very long life. He had dined with William Wilberforce who died in 1833, was a friend of Darwin's, displayed 'glee over Samuel Wilberforce's discomfiture by young Huxley' at the Oxford meetings of the British Association in 1860, and the next year entered upon his thirty-four years as professor of botany at Cambridge. His *Manual of British Botany*, first published in 1843, became a standard work and attained eventually a tenth edition in 1922.[1] Perhaps, too, we ought not to forget that S. R. Maitland, though he did not graduate, was a pioneer among medieval historians; and that Charles Merivale wrote his *History of the Romans under the Empire* after he retreated in 1849 from his fellowship to the college rectory at Lawford.

The new pathways which graduates were exploring, however, must not take us away from undergraduates. For the latter, around the mid-century, official teaching remained almost exclusively a matter of college provision. J. M. Wilson (B.A. 1859), indeed, was forbidden by his mathematical coach to attend professorial lectures 'as not bearing on the tripos sufficiently'.[2] College instruction, moreover, had virtually ceased to engage the statutory college lecturers. Their offices had become, as H. J. Roby said, 'mere names, for the most part without duty and without pay, like lifeless fossils which adorn their cabinets to some, curious antiquities to others, the speaking relics of a bygone era that was full of life'. In the place of the old lecturers stood the two tutors, each of whom appointed a staff of three mathematical and three classical lecturers. The only instruction common to the two tutorial 'sides' was that given by the Hebrew and Sadlerian lecturers, the latter teaching algebra to freshmen: consequently, men on different 'sides', though they met in hall and might meet socially, 'did not meet at lectures till the final preparation for the B.A. examination'.[1] Tutorial lecturers had often to show considerable versatility. G. D. Liveing, founder of the school of chemistry in Cambridge, lectured for two years in college on Paley's *Evidences* and classical lecturers were assumed 'to be perfectly competent to lecture on almost any subject...except mathematics'. This may explain why Merivale's lectures on the Greek Testament, Butler's *Analogy* and Plato's *Republic* did not particularly advance his reputation and why he appears even 'to have discoursed on Tacitus without increasing the inherent interest of his theme'.[2]

If this somewhat excessive disregard for specialization may have reduced the value of a good deal of college lecturing, its more serious defects attracted the attention of a number of observers. The practice of 'giving catechetical lectures to large classes of men of very unequal attainments was almost foredoomed to failure'; as T. G. Bonney noted, 'it wasted the time of the better men'. Additionally, as both Bonney and J. M. Wilson emphasize, college instruction resembled sixth-form lessons in school rather than lectures in the proper sense, but with this difference that the standard was lower than at a really good school. These defects made it necessary even for poll men to supplement official teaching with private coaching and similar assistance was indispensable for those who sought high honours. J. M. Wilson had recourse to this sort of additional instruction from one of the younger mathematical fellows, from young graduates in classics at St John's and Trinity, and from Stephen Parkinson, a fellow of St John's and one of the greatest mathematical coaches of the day. This development of private tuition was one which added substantially to the cost of a Cambridge education.[3]

If undergraduates had to incur new expenses, the range of social backgrounds from which they were recruited appears to have expanded once again. Taking the men admitted in 1842 as a sample,[1] there were no fewer gentlemen's sons in aggregate but, because total numbers had greatly increased, they were a smaller proportion of resident undergraduates. On the other hand, sons of professional men (especially of doctors, schoolmasters and men in public service) and of middle-class commercial and industrial families were more numerous both in aggregate and proportionately; while sons of artisans, shopkeepers and farmers were also more numerous than in the 1790's. Greater accessibility once more to men of relatively poor families is perhaps to be connected with the fact that the number of sizarships offered by the college had again increased. Bonney tells us that in the early 1850's there were about fifty-four sizars in residence: that is, about the same number as in 1750 and considerably more than in 1800.[2] The availability of this assistance enabled such men as J. C. Adams and J. W. Colenso (later to be bishop of Natal) to contemplate coming to Cambridge. The menial overtones of the sizar's status had disappeared towards the end of the eighteenth century; what remained was the financial and other assistance it offered to the poor student. Colenso tells us that, around 1832, it provided 'your dinner gratis, but you have a great chance of being allowed somewhat on the rent of your rooms.... We get our meat from the fellow's table, and though the joints are not very hot when they reach us, yet we manage to make very capital dinners.' A generation earlier, in 1805, Henry Kirke White had been even more satisfied: 'our dinners and suppers cost us nothing; and if a man choose to eat milk-breakfasts and go without tea, he may live absolutely for nothing; for his college emoluments will cover the rest of his expenses.'[3] Additionally, once a man had come up, there were over a hundred scholarships and exhibitions to be won. Many, it is true, were restricted to boys who had been to a particular school or who had been born in a particular county, and generally speaking their value was inadequate to cover the cost of maintenance and tuition. The fact remains, none the less, that a good deal was being done for the 'poor scholar'.[4]

The very fact that the college did so much, indeed, had a consequence of which there is evidence enough. Sons of wealthy families, inclined to regard a college education as a privilege of their station, were apt to despise their contemporaries endowed with less of this world's goods. One of William Henry Bateson's first services to a liberal cause was to fight, as an undergraduate in the 1830's, the rules which excluded sizars from the college cricket and boat clubs. His efforts did not erase the lines of social distinction, for they were evident enough twenty years later to the eye of Samuel Butler.[1] It did not help, as he pointed out, that 'the poorest undergraduates, who were dependent upon sizarships and scholarships for the means of taking their degrees', were concentrated in the Labyrinth (the old Hospital infirmary), with its 'dingy, tumble-down rooms'. 'They were rarely seen except in hall or chapel or at lecture, where their manners of feeding, praying and studying were considered alike objectionable.' The college might make much provision for the poor student, but his way was hard enough, and perhaps always had been, since first gentlemen came to the college.

There were other things in the 1840's which were characteristic of ways changing very slowly. The railway reached Cambridge only in 1845, so that a Cornishman like J. C. Adams spent his Christmas in college.[2] The hall was still heated by a charcoal brazier round which the fellows gathered before grace; and dinner had only recently declined to the 'peculiar hour' of 4 p.m. from 1 o'clock in the eighteenth century and 2 o'clock in 1799.[3] It consisted of a joint with vegetables and college-brewed beer, though sweets could be additionally paid for and private dinners might be ordered from the kitchen at heavy cost. The sole sports clubs were the Lady Margaret Boat Club and the cricket club, though men rode, drove in high dog-carts, played chess and cards, held wine parties after hall or lavish breakfast parties at which ham, pigeon pies and chops were served. The chapel, at which seven attendances each week were compulsory, provided choral services on Saturdays, Sundays and the evenings of Saints' days, for which the music was supplied by 'a peripatetic choir of men' which rushed from King's to Trinity and from Trinity to St John's, and was willing to add Jesus to its itinerary. The boy choristers continued to serve St John's and Trinity jointly. Not surprisingly, 'brevity was inevitable' in the services, a quality which may not always have seemed undesirable to those present by conscription.[1]

As for fellows, the old rules still prevailed. They had still, for the most part, to be celibate, to take orders and to proceed to the B.D. degree, though the last requirement was degenerating into a farce. John Eyton Bickersteth Mayor (B.A. 1848) observed that 'most men copied their Latin thesis from Limborch'; and that 'Dr Hymers moderated when my elder brother kept his thesis and told him he might talk at ease unless someone came in'.[2] These rules, however, compelled W. H. Miller, the crystallographer, to proceed M.D. in order to qualify for a medical fellowship and forced J. C. Adams to migrate to Pembroke when the college failed, to its 'deep regret', to persuade a law fellow to resign and so free a fellowship Adams might occupy without taking orders.[3] As in the past, too, not all of the fellows were resident. J. E. B. Mayor spent his first four years as a fellow teaching at Marlborough, and the tenure of his brother, Robert Bickersteth Mayor, coincided exactly with his time as an assistant master at Rugby (1858–64). Even much later than this, Sir John Eliot was a fellow from 1869, until he married in 1877, while resident in India laying the foundations of his distinguished career as a meteorologist and educationist.[4] Most fellows, however, as they had done from the beginning, were more likely to find their ultimate retreat in a parsonage. Some things, in fact, about the college of the mid-nineteenth century would not have seemed too strange to Samuel Ogden.

III

More far-reaching changes were soon to come and a convenient point of departure for the new age is the appointment of William Henry Bateson as senior bursar in 1846. During the next eleven years he was responsible for important alterations in financial policy. The old system of beneficial leases and periodic fines was given up and estates were let at rack-rent;

expenditure on improvements was stepped up with a consequent increase in the letting value of farms; and in general, favoured by agricultural prosperity, the college revenue increased. The fellows, after initial sacrifices, reaped the benefit, the dividend rising from £130 in 1846 to £180 in 1857. In that year Bateson became master, but the policy he had inaugurated was continued and extended in circumstances which remained propitious. Worse land was sold and better bought, the college's Kentish Town property was developed as a building estate and the scaling up of farm rents to economic levels was completed. Income from rents rose from £17,000 in 1857 to £32,000 in 1881 and total gross revenue from £30,000 to £46,000 in the same period. This enabled the fellows' dividend to be raised to £300 in the years 1872–8; but it also provided resources for financing out of general revenue, as well as from fees paid by undergraduates, an ampler educational provision by the college.

Reforms in estate-management absorbed only a part of Bateson's energies.[1] He was a member of the syndicate set up in 1849 to revise the statutes of the university; he was secretary of the royal commission on the affairs of the colleges and the university in 1850–2; and he was a commissioner for the later enquiry in 1874. This is no place to speak of his part in university affairs, but of his central place in the reform of the college there can be no question. He played a prominent part in the revision of the statutes in 1848; he was a protagonist of the changes which the commission of 1850 made necessary or desirable; the revision of the statutes in 1857–60 took place under him as master; and much of the code of 1882 had been worked out before his death. These successive acts of legislation mark the direction and measure the rate of change.

In 1847 the initiative was taken by the college. It proposed, as part of a general movement in Cambridge to stave off threatened government intervention, to revise its statutes. The proposal did not pass unchallenged. Thomas Crick, who had been president from 1839 to 1846, appealed to the visitor on the ground that the oath fellows took to uphold the statutes precluded any attempt to alter them. The bishop of Ely, however, did not support this extremity of conservative logic, particularly since he was assured that the college intended to adhere to the spirit of its statutes and even to their 'very form and language'.[1]

He had not been misinformed. The most novel thing about the 1848 statutes was that they were printed and a copy was given to every fellow. They were, however, still in Latin, repeated *verbatim* much of the Elizabethan code and modified it only to the extent that they made statutory rules somewhat more conformable with customary practice. The power of tutors to engage other fellows to assist with the instruction of their 'sides' was recognized, though only as an addendum to the Elizabethan statute on the office of tutor (when it was one incumbent upon all fellows and very different from the tutorship of the nineteenth century). Similarly, the statutes provided, as warranted by established custom, that dividend should be paid to the fellows from the college balances (*excrescentiae*) and that the surplus revenue from the corn rents should be shared between master and fellows in the form of the payment known as *praeter*. It is hard to see, however, that the new code was, as the college claimed, 'more conformable to the present state of learning and science'; and the coolness towards reform in St John's is some indication of the need for a royal commission.[2]

That commission when it came, and the provision it made for new studies in the university, made much more far-reaching changes necessary; but these were also brought about by the emergence of a reforming group in the college under the leadership of Bateson, Liveing, J. E. B. Mayor and H. J. Roby.[3] Indeed, the first advances upon the position taken up in 1848 were made by college order. In 1853 the old autonomy of the two tutorial 'sides' was modified, there was some attempt to divide mathematical lecture classes according to 'ability and proficiency', four additional college lecturers were appointed (two of them to teach the new subjects, moral and natural sciences), and lecturers were guaranteed a salary of £120 a year, the college agreeing to supplement from general revenue tuition fees received from pupils to make up this amount.[4] The natural sciences lectureship went to G. D. Liveing. He had, in the previous year, fitted up a chemistry laboratory at his own expense in Slaughter House Lane (now

Corn Exchange Street), but the college, at Bateson's instance, now built him a laboratory behind new court where the first college baths were to be many years later. He was subsequently retained as director of the laboratory when he married and forfeited his fellowship, and when he became professor of chemistry in 1861 because, until 1888, there was no other laboratory in which he could give instruction. In his own words, this was 'the first seed sown towards the growth of a large chemical school' in Cambridge.[1]

There remained, however, much to do and in 1857 H. J. Roby continued to be critical of the system of tutorial instruction and of government by the eight senior fellows, of whom never more than five and sometimes only two were in residence.[2] But over against Roby and his friends stood others with less forward views. Even a decade later than this, W. E. Heitland considered that the college was controlled by 'a narrow minded and bigoted clique' and that the damage which might have been done was only mitigated by Bateson's skill in managing 'an untoward crew of seniors'.[3] For all their resistance, however, change had to come and any lack of impetus within the college was balanced by compulsions acting from without.

Those compulsions arose from the work of the royal commission of 1850, which reported in 1852 on the 'state, discipline, studies and revenues' of the university and colleges. There was no haste in Cambridge to act upon this report, with the consequence that the Cambridge University Act of 1856 empowered eight commissioners to supervise (and after 1 January 1858 to undertake) the revision of college and university statutes. The college, therefore, had no choice but to work out, between 1857 and 1860, new statutes. Compared with those of 1848 they introduced radical innovations. The Elizabethan code was virtually abandoned *in toto* and with it disappeared those ancient offices which had degenerated into 'lifeless fossils'. Other attributes of old times were transformed root and branch. From some points of view the most important change was that merging into the general property of the college the numerous separate endowments (including the Platt endowment) of fellowships and scholarships, exception being made only for some funds maintaining awards attached to certain schools, which were retained to support closed exhibitions. In consequence, the Platt fellows were given parity of stipend and standing with other fellows; all county and other qualifications for fellowships and scholarships were abolished; the value of scholarships was somewhat increased; and four scholarships were reserved each year for award to men who had not yet, or who had only just, come into residence (the first beginnings of entrance scholarships). 'The more conservative members' defeated proposals to abandon generally the rules that fellows must be ordained and celibate; but professors and university lecturers could be elected to fellowships without coming under these conditions and college officers were no longer obliged to be in orders.[1]

The new statutes were a substantial breach in the old order and change was pushed forward by the college itself in the ensuing period. The educational gulf between the tutorial 'sides' was closed in 1860, when three tutors were appointed and also ten *college* lecturers, whose classes were to be open to all. In the same year, the examinations for open and foundation scholarships gave parity to classics and mathematics, for a candidate could be elected for proficiency in either subject considered independently. An open exhibition in natural sciences was established in 1868 and by 1880 fourteen open awards were being offered, which also included an exhibition in oriental languages.[2] By that time, too, E. H. Palmer had been elected a fellow for his proficiency as an oriental linguist and in spite of a third class in the classical tripos; and A. H. Garrod had become in 1871 the first fellow who had graduated by way of the natural sciences tripos.[3] There is other evidence of a new diversity of studies. In 1875 there were college examinations in mathematics, classics, theology, natural sciences, moral science and the combined subject law and history.[4] Bryan Walker was imported from Corpus Christi college in 1869 to lecture in law and by 1881 Donald MacAlister was lecturing on medical subjects in the college of Heberden and Haviland. By that time, too, T. G. Bonney had taught geology in St John's; J. E. Marr (later Woodwardian professor of geology), W. J. Sollas (later professor of geology at Oxford) and Jethro Teall (later director of the Geological Survey) had already graduated; and Alfred

Harker, who was to establish the teaching of petrology in Cambridge on a firm basis, would do so in 1882. The breadth of moral science ought also not to be forgotten. The college lecturers in this subject included H. S. Foxwell and Alfred Marshall, both economists of distinction and the latter the true progenitor of the modern school of economics in Cambridge.[1]

To put these tendencies another way, clearly the old rule of mathematics, or of mathematics and classics together, was breaking down. By 1880 no less than eight triposes were available. At the same time, the rush of Johnians to take advantage of new opportunities must not be exaggerated. Only seventy-five out of 194 freshmen coming up in 1876 and 1877[2] figured in the tripos lists at all. Of the rest, some took no degree and others, because they were genuinely stupid or did little work in Heitland's view, were content to be 'poll men'.[3] Moreover, even among honours men, the new triposes had as yet gained little popularity. Only four of the freshmen of 1876–7 took moral science, nine natural sciences, eight theology, seven law and two history; more than half were still engaged in mathematics (30) and classics (15). The latter study, at least, had improved its position sufficiently for the years round 1870 to be considered the 'golden age of Johnian classics'. If so, the gold came chiefly from a single mine: from Shrewsbury, the school which produced Heitland, Henry Wace (like Heitland senior classic, but also a rugby 'blue' and a soccer international) and T. E. Page, whose editorship of the Loeb classical texts was marked by a steady flow of gifts to the college library.[4]

If new opportunities were not always seized, neither did old deficiencies in the college lecturing system entirely disappear; for human frailties and the system itself stood in the way. Some of the deficiencies were personified by Isaac Todhunter. Undoubtedly he was a character: 'quaint, crochety, sour, uncouth, surrounded by cats and canaries'. Much of his time was absorbed by private coaching and he worked 'with true mathematical precision: chapel at 7.30, pupils from 8.15 until 3 o'clock, a walk which never varied until dinner at 4, and from 5.30 to 10 another stream of pupils'. There can be no question of his devotion to mathematics, though there may be an element of myth in the tale that he introduced his wife to Hamilton's Quaternions on their honeymoon. Certainly he was a successful teacher; and it can be accounted in part his achievement that Leslie Stephen, who came to him from Trinity Hall, turned himself into a reasonable mathematician. His college lectures in the 1870's, however, still smacked of the schoolroom. 'His method consisted in dictating twelve questions.... Having done this he retired to an inner room, ... reappearing towards the end of an hour to see what we had done.... His criticism was chiefly directed to the handwriting.'

There were other faults in the system, noted by those who were submitted to it. Serious students were compelled, under penalty of being gated, to attend quite elementary lectures. This compulsion was not made more bearable in the early 1870's when, with one or two exceptions, the Johnian lecturers at first refused to take any notice of changes in the syllabus for the mathematical tripos. Sometimes, on the other hand, the trouble was one of manner rather than matter. Richard Pendlebury in mathematics, for example, or J. E. B. Mayor in classics, only prepared their lectures 'so far as to set the tap running'. The results were not necessarily uninstructive, depending to some extent upon the audience; but it is hard to avoid the impression that a good deal must have been lost when Mayor lectured to mathematical men on the Greek and Latin texts for the previous examination, then taken during residence, and 'poured out...a torrent of learning which would...have overwhelmed a senior classic'.[1] The conscientious provision of college lectures for 'poll men', too, as Heitland pointed out, was a 'wasteful failure', for the idle needed 'dry-nursing' at the last moment and the stupid all the time, functions which were far better fulfilled by private coaches. J. W. Pieters, who is said to have got his nickname 'plucky' for his courage in coaching for the ordinary degree men regarded as hopeless by others, probably did much more for them than the college lecturers. Coaches were not less necessary for honours men, if only because, as courses became more diverse, even a large college could not give sufficient attention to individuals.[2] It is true that, in this connection, an improvement was creeping in under an impulse which came originally from Trinity in the 1860's. By 1872, St John's was co-operating with a number of other colleges in intercollegiate lecturing arrangements for classics, natural sciences and moral science; and in 1878 some of the college's mathematical lectures were thrown open. There was still far to go, however, before Powell's ideal of collegiate autonomy disappeared.[1]

There had been, in the meantime, other and substantial changes. The royal commission of 1850 was cautiously liberal about the religious restrictions which made colleges all but Anglican preserves; and the Cambridge University Act of 1856 exempted from the obligation to subscribe to the Thirty-nine Articles all those taking degrees other than in divinity. On the other hand, only Anglicans could be members of the senate or hold offices previously restricted to Anglicans. Thus, while dissenters might now take degrees, they were still excluded from fellowships and from college and university posts. A movement for further relaxation developed slowly; but a petition from Cambridge in 1869, with influential support including that of Bateson, led directly to the statute of 1871 abolishing religious tests for all save heads of houses and candidates for degrees in divinity. In this manner dissenters and those without religious affiliations gained parity of opportunity in the college with Anglicans. It need hardly be said that the change did not meet with universal approbation. J. S. Wood, who became president at the very time that the act of 1871 became law, thundered against a measure which turned colleges into 'chance medleys of churchmen, dissenters and unbelievers,...bodies alien to the Church of England, alien to the church of Christ'. Religious passions were stirred and T. G. Bonney and G. F. Reyner (B.A. 1839 and senior bursar 1857–76) swapped sermons in the chapel in defence of latitudinarian and more traditional views respectively, creating an atmosphere which made it necessary for sermons to be discontinued for some years. Perhaps it mattered little if Heitland was right, that 'in order to get spiritual nourishment from the chapel services, you had to take it in with you and in some highly developed form'.[2]

Bateson could not compose these quarrels, but neither could those who looked to the past prevent further changes. In the 1870's the affairs of the university and colleges were again submitted to scrutiny by government commissions and the Universities of Oxford and Cambridge Act of 1877 again nominated commissioners to revise university and college statutes. The new statutes of St John's, finally approved in 1882, reflected the general principles upon which the commissioners insisted. They abolished the requirements that fellows should take orders and remain celibate and that the master must be in holy orders. They replaced the seniority by a college council consisting of the master and twelve other members chosen by the body of the fellows. They made provision for general meetings of the fellows. They limited the tenure of fellowships to six years, save where the holder of a fellowship qualified for extension on the ground that he was an officer or lecturer of the college or the university. They provided for a contribution from college funds towards the educational expenditure of the university, an obligation which the college had refused to entertain in 1860.[1]

These statutes were a more radical break with the past than those of a generation earlier. They set a term to the original idea of the college as a school of theology with monastic overtones. A fellowship was no longer the last stage in training for the priesthood (a notion itself which had long been anachronistic): it was an office, in principle, for a man engaged in a career of teaching and research. Further, the connection established in the 1850's between colleges and the university was strengthened. Between the sixteenth and the mid-nineteenth centuries the university's contribution to the teaching of undergraduates had been in the main a matter for professors, who were ineligible for fellowships and whose duties often sat lightly on them. Between 1850 and 1882 that situation was transformed by increasing the number of professors who actually taught, by creating a staff of university lecturers, by making professors and lecturers eligible for college fellowships and by instituting college contributions to university funds. In this way collegiate autonomy was broken down and conditions were created which enabled the university, for the first time since the sixteenth century, to bulk larger than the colleges. On the other hand, the links between university and colleges, which university officers occupying

V. THE CHAPEL AND MASTER'S LODGE, FIRST COURT, *c.* 1865

college fellowships represented, prevented the balance from shifting in a wholly one-sided manner. In due course, though it took time, a new, co-operative pattern was established which is the basis of modern practice.

By comparison, alterations in the physical appearance of the college in Bateson's age were perhaps of smaller significance. The major monument, here, was the new chapel consecrated on 12 May 1869 and constituting in William Selwyn's view a 'sermon in stones'. Bonney, on the other hand, considered it to be from first to last a failure and others have been critical of Sir George Gilbert Scott's achievement (though, in fairness to Scott, it ought to be said that his proposal was to restore and if necessary to extend the old chapel, and that the policy actually pursued was laid down by 'the dominant party among the fellows').[1] That policy involved the demolition of the old chapel and the Labyrinth (though the loss of the latter need cause no tears), the final destruction of the architectural integrity of first court and the erection of an edifice which is 'alien in the community of college buildings'. Opportunity was also taken to enlarge the hall, adding the second oriel window and some forty feet to its length, a work in which 'Scott's flair for reproduction of the antique can nowhere have been more happily used'. At the same time, since demolition of the old chapel range and the extension of the hall robbed the master of much of his lodge and the fellows of their combination room, it was considered necessary to build the present master's lodge which freed the long gallery, with its partitions removed, to serve as a combination room. All in all, the cost of these operations was £78,000, £40,000 of which was met from James Wood's bequest and from donations by members of the college in roughly equal proportions. The balance had to be cleared over a period from general revenue and by the time the debt was extinguished in 1896 interest charges had amounted to over £20,000.

The building of the new chapel provided a natural occasion for reconstructing and enlarging the organ, and other improvements were made to it in 1889 and 1902. Further, the pulling down of the Labyrinth reduced living accommodation precisely at a time when a greater diversity of college lectures was also calling for more teaching space. It was to solve these problems that, in 1885–8, the 'inoffensive neo-Tudor' western range of chapel court (a motion to call it north wing was lost by five votes to four) was built after the design of F.C. Penrose and in a brick unfortunately harsh in line and colour. It provided lecture rooms and a physics laboratory on the ground floor, with sets of rooms above, at a cost of £10,000. This charge was met from existing balances and the building, of course, produced an immediate return in the form of room rents.[1]

Joseph Bickersteth Mayor, yet another brother of J. E. B. Mayor, looking back in 1877 upon the preceding quarter of a century, was able to observe, not without justice, that 'everywhere there is movement, growth, expansion.... Improvement externally in the widespread influence of the university;... and improvement internally in regard to the range of studies, the methods of teaching, the position of the teacher and the encouragement offered to students.'[2] 'Reading men' were still, perhaps, somewhat rarer than many might desire and social distinctions were still recognized with something of the frankness characteristic of Samuel Butler's undergraduate days.[3] On the other hand, the catchment area from which the college recruited its students in 1881[4] was larger than it had been in 1842, just as in 1842 it had been larger than in 1790. The majority of undergraduates were still sons of professional men: but sons of lawyers, doctors, men in government service, artists, architects and so forth now outnumbered in aggregate sons of clergymen (even including the sons of nonconformist pastors). There were fewer sons of landed gentlemen, but more sons of businessmen (now as numerous as sons of the clergy). There were also men who came from families of no great wealth and particularly noticeable is the number of men whose fathers were engaged in 'white collar' occupations—were clerks, cashiers and the like. The new open scholarships probably contributed to the increasing diversity in the background of undergraduates.

If opportunities to come up were being enlarged, so were opportunities for those going down. For the most part the college continued to train men for the professions, but this was a time in which the range of professions was expanding. In some respects, moreover, the college was offering positive assistance towards launching its graduates in a professional career. The McMahon law studentships were founded in 1864 to aid those wishing to read for the bar at an Inn of Court or to serve an attorney or solicitor under articles. The first election was made the following year and the successful candidate was H. F. Pooley, later assistant secretary of the Board of Education. Professions old and new, however, might take men much further afield than that. Bishop Colenso's work was done in Natal and Johnians were particularly prominent in the early development of New Zealand, where George Augustus Selwyn served as bishop and William Martin as chief justice. St John's, too, gave special encouragement to candidates for the Indian Civil Service, a fact which also helped to bring a number of Indians to the college.[1] At the same time, other and very different openings were beginning to attract graduates. Various members of the Hoare family and William Cunliffe Brookes went back to their family banking firms; Francis Bashford, a contemporary of J. C. Adams, was a railway surveyor and then, at the age of forty-two, was dug out of a college living to act as scientific adviser to the army on the ballistics of the rifle; and Sir Charles Parsons, son of an earl and eleventh wrangler in 1877, became, in Sir Humphry Rolleston's view, 'the greatest engineer since James Watt' and the first member of that profession to receive the O.M. Even H. J. Roby, the college reformer of the 1850's, joined in due course the cotton firm owned by his wife's relatives and lived to be a prominent figure in industrial Manchester. The college was attracting new sorts of men: but it was also supplying new sorts of men to shoulder the responsibilities of industrial England.[2]

If this was one feature of the college in the 1880's which would not seem strange to us, it was not the only one. Growing numbers in the nineteenth century made it normal for most men to spend some part of their time out of college. In 1851 133 out of 351 undergraduates in residence were in lodgings and the same was true of 104 out of 215 first- and second-year men in 1879.[3] The college buildings were as they were to be until 1940. Courses of study were moving towards their modern diversity. The high table was beginning to lose its clerical aspect. By 1876 there were two halls, at 5.30 and 7.15,[4] though first lectures at 8 a.m. might alarm the modern undergraduate and reliance upon one's tutor in time of sickness might seem less satisfactory than the modern nurse and sick-bay.[1] On the other hand, the range of recreations was assuming familiar dimensions. The first steps towards creating the sports field were taken in 1858 and most of the present sports clubs had been founded by 1880.[2] G. M. Garret, soon after becoming organist in 1857, established a musical society to which, in 1868, the majority of resident members subscribed;[3] and the *Eagle* was founded in 1858 to give scope, as it has done ever since, to undergraduate and some graduate scribblers, both willing and conscribed. In all this there is more than familiarity: there is a new breadth to the activities which the college permitted or encouraged its members to pursue.

These, then, were some of the characteristics of the age of Bateson. He carried through no revolution: if there were features of the college in 1881 which would be recognizable to us, there were others which would not have seemed strange to the young J. C. Adams or the young Samuel Butler. What Bateson did do, however, was to liberalize the college in the best high Victorian sense. He was engaged on that work right to the end of his life, as an architect of university reform and as chairman of college meetings working out the implications of university reform for the domestic rules of St John's. We are told that, in this latter capacity, 'he always showed a special interest in referring to the precedents of the last revision of the college statutes'.[4] This is testimony to the continuity which marked his work, the outcome of which was to turn an eminently conservative into a more liberal community, using those words with an application to mental and spiritual (and not mere political) attitudes. To put the matter another way, he laid the foundations of the modern college and he laid them firmly and well. For that he will be remembered among those masters who have served it with distinction.

V

THE PRE-WAR YEARS AND WAR-TIME (1882-1918)

BATESON died on 27 March 1881 and soon 'speculation was very rife as to the new master.[1] In the event the choice of the fellows was Dr Charles Taylor. He had much in common with many of his predecessors. As an undergraduate his studies had been in mathematics and classics and he then proceeded in 1863 to a first class in the theological examination, presaging his future distinction as 'one of the masters of Rabbinic learning'. He became a fellow in 1864, took orders in accordance with the statutes and served the college as lecturer in theology. At the same time, he had already displayed a capacity for affairs as well as scholarship before 1881. He served on the college committees considering the revision of the statutes in 1887–8 and, with Bateson and T. G. Bonney, was chosen in 1879 one of the representatives of St John's to deal on its behalf with the commissioners nominated in the act of 1877. From the beginning, therefore, 'he found himself in the full current of an epoch of change'. He might have 'no reforming tendencies of his own' and 'a short way with visionary and unpractical schemes'; but 'he was always ready to support proposals for reform, provided they were well thought out'. Circumstances being what they were, proposals for reform were frequent enough from the beginning to the end of his time.[2]

To that extent, then, there was continuity between Bateson's age and the time of Taylor; and some changes begun under Taylor were carried a small way further after R. F. Scott succeeded him in 1908 and before the outbreak of war in 1914 extensively disrupted the life of the college. Scott, however, was in some respects a very different figure from any of his predecessors. He had had some schooling in Germany; he had been a student at King's College, London, before he came up to read mathematics at St John's; and he was called to the bar from Lincoln's Inn before he returned to the college as its man of affairs in a time of need. He was the first Scot and, more significantly, the first layman to be master; and his rule extended to 1933, thus taking in the difficult time of the first war and the new era of reform which followed. He was the first master of St John's to be accorded the accolade of knighthood.[1] If Scott was, in some ways, a new sort of master, that is not to say that his accession in 1908 marked a fundamental change. He began to play a significant directing part in the college's affairs from the time he came back as senior bursar in 1883; and it was the outbreak of the world war in 1914, rather than the change of masters in 1908, which was a real dividing line in the history of the modern college.

I

When Taylor followed Bateson the first task which had to be completed was the working out of the new statutes of 1882. This code, however, was the final monument of Bateson's age and it has been treated as such; but there were other practical problems demanding the immediate attention of the new master. Most urgent was a serious crisis in the college's financial affairs. The prosperity of agriculture had collapsed in the late 1870's; already in 1880 the fellowship dividend had been brought down from £300 to £290 and in 1883 J. W. Pieters resigned the senior bursarship in disappointment at what looked like consistent failure.[2] This was the point at which R. F. Scott came back to take his place and he had to report at once upon the 'bankrupt condition of sundry college tenants'. For the next dozen years or so the situation continued to deteriorate. Arrears accumulated, rents had to be scaled down, some farms could not be let and had to be kept in hand and run at a loss. By 1896 external revenue had fallen by one third; many fellowships had been left vacant; the Somerset exhibitions could sometimes not be filled because the fund was insolvent; and the fellowship dividend was down to £80.[3] For all the improvements in management which Bateson had made, the fact was that his policy of relying exclusively upon the fortunes of agriculture had been found wanting. For the last two decades of the nineteenth century and perhaps for longer, financial difficulties limited the college's capacity to fulfil its educational responsibilities.

Recovery inevitably required time. A wider spread of investments was clearly necessary, but there were obstacles to that apart from conservative desires not to abandon old ways. In 1895 an approach was made to the Board of Agriculture 'on the question of the general policy of selling un-desirable farms'; but the Board, while expressing willingness to consider particular applications, refused any general pronouncement.[1] Over the long term, however, by means of particular applications, some properties which gave a low return or were difficult to manage were sold. In 1918 revenue from agricultural land, though somewhat higher than it had been in 1896 in consequence of a recovery in farming fortunes, constituted a smaller proportion of the college's external income. Interest on securities, though still relatively small, had been increased considerably; and revenues from houses at rack-rent and from building leases had grown still more notably. This had mainly been achieved by developing, in line with experience gained earlier in the Kentish Town estate, the Grange Road and Madingley Road areas in Cambridge from about 1885 and property at Sunningdale after 1899.

These policies prosecuted by R. F. Scott enabled the college to weather a serious financial crisis. Investments were ultimately more widely spread than at any time in the past. It became possible to increase the fellowship dividend by stages between 1896 and 1904 to £200, at which figure it remained for the next two decades. By 1918 external revenue had almost regained its 1880 level, although the fall in the value of money made that recovery less complete than the figures suggest. At least, however, the downward trend of the late nineteenth century was reversed.

Financial crisis and recovery have more than an economic significance. The generation or two prior to 1914 witnessed a development and expansion of higher education in Britain which Heitland, towards the end of his life, called 'a splendid onward movement'.[2] One index of it was the growing number of students in old and new universities and colleges. At Cambridge, the number of men matriculating each year increased between 1880 and 1907 by nearly one half. At this very time, however, St John's entered into a period of recession: its annual entry fell from 104 in 1880 to seventy-three in 1900 and rose only very slowly in the following decade. On the eve of the First World War there were only about 274 junior members in residence.[1] During the same period financial aid offered to undergraduates also contracted. In 1880 the figure stood at £6700, but it fell to £3900 in 1896 and had crept up again only to £4700 in 1910. While other causes may have been at work, it looks as though financial stringency helped to explain the recession of numbers at St John's. For the time being the college could no longer offer financial inducements on the old scale to the poorer man; and its teaching provision, still mainly a collegiate matter, was probably also constricted by economic difficulties.

Numbers of undergraduates and the gross total of the scholarship fund, however, were not necessarily the only things which mattered. Partly in consequence of the conversion, in name or in fact, of about one third of the college's sizarships into entrance exhibitions, a larger proportion of the scholarship fund came to be used for open awards offered for competition among men who had not yet come into residence.[2] In 1882 there were eleven open awards, but this figure had increased to twenty-seven in 1912 and some of them were of somewhat higher value than they had been formerly. More and better awards probably helped to attract to the college able men whose means were small, to that extent offsetting the effects of a decrease in the total assistance available to undergraduates. Such a supposition has the support of J. R. Tanner's contention in 1889 that entrance scholarships were a magnet to promising students. For this reason he wished for open awards to be made available to historians;[3] and, in his desire to extend the range of subjects covered by the open scholarship examination, Tanner was representative of an effective body of opinion in the college. In 1882, apart from one exhibition in Hebrew and another in natural sciences, all the open awards had been for candidates in classics or mathematics. In 1912, on the other hand, while nine awards were made in classics and five in mathematics, there were also one in Hebrew, nine in natural sciences, two in history and one in modern languages.[1]

A similar and increasing diversity of talents came also to be rewarded for achievements while in residence. First- and second-year men studying subjects other than classics and mathematics were made eligible for Wright's prizes in 1885;[2] and scholarships and exhibitions, awarded for merit displayed in examinations by resident undergraduates, were offered in a lengthening list of subjects. This point can be illustrated by a glance at the distribution according to subject studied of the scholars and exhibitioners of the college at two different points of time.

Subject	Numbers	
	1886–7	1909–10
Mathematics	30	21
Classics	12	24
Hebrew	—	1
Natural Sciences	12	19
Theology	2	3
Law	—	1
History	—	3
Modern Languages	—	5
Economics	—	2

A feature of these figures is the growing prominence of natural scientists, including medical students (the popularity of medicine was a matter for comment in 1884 and was something which owed a good deal to Dr D. MacAlister).[3] Technology, too, had made its appearance, for one mechanical scientist was awarded an exhibition in 1895 and two were similarly rewarded in 1896. At the same time, the newer arts subjects were also gaining in popularity: of those who came up in 1909 to read honours courses, about as many were engaged in study for the historical tripos as in classics or mathematics. From one point of view, of course, this is merely to say that the range of studies made available by the university was expanding rapidly at this time; but Johnians took advantage of this fact and were positively encouraged to do so by the college's policy in regard to scholarships and prizes.

This was not the only feature of college educational policy at this time. A good deal of attention was also devoted to the standard of effort which ought to be expected of undergraduates.[1] As tutor, W. E. Heitland might permit A. M. Mond, the future Lord Melchett, 'to let his activities in Union debates absorb the attention due to chemistry', and his tolerance was perhaps justified by the future career of that captain of industry. On the other hand, Heitland was convinced that, 'unless a young man has something like genius and is free from financial anxieties, perhaps he had better travel by the common highway of a degree'.[2] If Lord Melchett did not travel by that way, it was the college's policy to insist that most men did and that far more men than in the past should be expected to aim at an honours degree. Very few of the men who came up in 1909 did not graduate and at least two thirds of them did so with honours, a notable advance on the position in 1880. If numbers were smaller than in Bateson's time, quality would seem to be higher.

The diversity of talent which the college sought to attract was increased in other ways. Perhaps following the tradition already established in the eighteenth century, it was hospitable to men from overseas. As early as 1877 Dairoki Kikuchi, a notable figure in the westernization of Japan, had graduated from St John's, and at the end of the nineteenth century the college was extending a particular welcome to colonial and commonwealth students. They included some men of distinction: Grafton Elliot-Smith, the Australian anatomist and anthropologist; and R. P. Paranjpye, bracketed senior wrangler in 1899, a fellow in 1901 (the first Indian to be elected by any college in Oxford or Cambridge) and later, in recognition of his outstanding career in the educational and public life of his own country, an honorary fellow. In this respect, too, the college proceeded with intent and deliberation. A scholarship was instituted in 1906 for students from Canadian universities and in 1914 an exhibition open to candidates from any university or college in the British Empire.[3]

The policy of drawing men from overseas was closely associated with another: the precocious willingness of St John's, noted by Sir J. J. Thomson, to sponsor graduate students drawn from other universities as well as from its own members.[1] Regulations for advanced students, precursors of the later research students, were drawn up by the college council in 1896;[2] and under them, among others, Elliot-Smith was brought from the University of Sydney and J. M. Wordie, later to be master, from Glasgow University. Funds were also acquired which enabled the college to aid men engaged in post-graduate studies. Some of them were already old, for the Naden divinity studentships went back to 1712 and the Ann Fry Hebrew student-ship was established in 1844; but two Hutchinson studentships in natural sciences or in Semitic or Indian languages were added in 1885, and a Slater studentship in physical and natural sciences in 1912. Not only had the seg-ment of the college engaged in post-graduate research made its appearance by 1914; resources enabling the college to offer specific encouragement to scientific research had been made available, if only on a modest scale.

The changes in educational policy between 1881 and 1914, made quietly and without drama, were important features of Dr Taylor's mastership and of the early years of Sir Robert Scott. They are also related to more general changes in English society and the college's function in it. Not unnatur-ally, in an age of agricultural depression, sons of the landed gentry were a less prominent element among undergraduates at St John's than in many past ages. Proportionately, too, the college bred fewer clergymen. On the other hand, trends which had been evident earlier became more marked. Relatively more Johnians passed into the medical and legal professions and into the public service—the home civil, the Indian and the colonial services as well as the armed forces. A large number, too, became schoolmasters and not a few entered the comparatively new profession of university teaching. In the year 1899 alone, the *Eagle* recorded the election to chairs at Oxford of two Johnians who had previously been professors at London and Aberdeen; and other academic appointments were filled by members of the college at Liverpool, Manchester, Edinburgh, Cape Town, Winnipeg and Wellington (New Zealand). Not less significant was the increasing flow into business and industry. In 1900 (the year in which Miles Walker, a scholar of St John's, was engaged as an electrical engineer by the Westinghouse Company of Pittsburg, U.S.A.), the college gave financial support to the Cambridge Appointments Association, parent of the modern Appointments Board. The object of the Association was to advise applicants for employment, not only in the older professions, but in banking, railways, ship-building, commerce, industry, engineering and agriculture.[1] The college was making a more varied educational provision for its undergraduates in the years before 1914; it was also training them for a greater variety of occupations.

II

New statutes and curricular changes also worked changes in the fellowship of the college. The statutes of 1882 were, in this respect, a watershed. Before they were promulgated a fellowship had been, in effect, a prize and the main qualification had been distinction in university examinations. For that reason, university examinations being what they were, under-graduate proficiency in mathematics and to a lesser extent classics had been somewhat excessive advantages. Once a man became a fellow, moreover, there was no obligation of residence or duty and no limit to tenure save that implied by a willingness to be ordained and to refrain from matrimony. These last characteristics were altogether changed by the 1882 statutes. The obligation to be ordained and celibate was swept away; the initial period of tenure was reduced to six years and further reduced to three in 1912; and renewal thereafter was made normally contingent upon occupation of a college or university office. A fellowship, therefore, ceased to be a fee simple: it became instead something for which a man qualified by active participation in the educational life of Cambridge and its colleges.

The changes made in 1882 were only a beginning. A college order of 1883 decreed that, in future, electors to fellowships would take account, in addition to the examination records of candidates, of any writings or dis-sertations which they might submit. It was recognized, in other words, that the qualification for a fellowship should be a capacity for research as well as undergraduate proficiency, a principle which made broader the way for scholars of greater diversity. E. J. Rapson, for example, was elected in 1887, not only because he had displayed distinction in the classical tripos,

VI. THE COLLEGE CHEMISTRY LABORATORY, CLOSED 1914

but also for the merit exhibited by his dissertations on Indian languages and history; and in the following year Thomas Darlington became a fellow, having submitted writings upon the folk-speech of southern Cheshire.[1] We may not say, when we remember E. H. Palmer, that such men might not have been elected even in the old days. This much is clear, however, that the new procedure enabled specific account to be taken of a more varied range of talents and that the modern notion of research fellowships was taking shape.

The requirements of college teaching also made for more diversity among the fellows. Although university provision had increased, it was still assumed in 1882 that the teaching of undergraduates was mainly a task for college lecturers supplemented by private coaches. As new subjects entered the university curriculum, therefore, there was a call for new college lectureships, some of which qualified their holders for fellowships. In the year 1884, for example, J. R. Tanner and J. B. Mullinger were appointed to lecture in history and S. L. Hart in physics, the college providing a laboratory for him in third court before new accommodation for it in chapel court was ready.[2] Later, Alfred Harker held his only college office as physics lecturer and lectures were provided in French, at first for the previous examination and afterwards for the modern languages tripos.[3]

These examples might easily be multiplied, but it is also important to notice that college provision might have to face competition from the university. In the Easter term of 1887 Tanner found that 'the arrangements made by the Historical Board left him no subject to lecture on';[4] and it was for a like reason that the college physics laboratory was closed in 1894, freeing Harker to devote himself to his geological work, and the chemistry laboratory in 1914. Further, the tendency, already evident in the 1870's, was growing to use college staffs more economically by making intercollegiate arrangements both for lecturing and examining; and by 1905 Dr H. F. Baker was quite clear in his mind that 'time must bring a more intimate intercollegiate organization of mathematical lectures'.[5] What applied in mathematics applied obviously in other subjects and, if collegiate provision was in this manner losing ground to intercollegiate arrangements, perhaps there was some inevitability that the latter would shade off into university provision.

While in this way the college was losing some of its autonomy, it was working towards a new type of educational provision: individual supervision of undergraduates taken singly or in small groups. This had been, in the past, the province of the private coaches, still at first a familiar feature of the Cambridge scene, particularly for mathematicians. Famous among them was R. R. Webb, college lecturer from 1877 to 1911, who sometimes coached for sixty hours a week. Some thought, however, parodying a well-known hymn, that the palm ought to be awarded to A. E. H. Love, who became professor of natural philosophy at Oxford in 1899:

> Herman, Love and Webb we see
> Strive in keenest rivalry,
> But the greatest of the three
> And the best is Love.[1]

As late as 1905 H. F. Baker declared that the majority of mathematical men coached, though by that time the supervision system was spreading rapidly. When E. A. Benians came up in 1899, the history lecturers provided individual teaching weekly during a man's first term and more occasionally thereafter for the rest of his first year.[2] The key date, however, is perhaps 1901. In that year Dr D. MacAlister's college lectureship in medicine was abolished, on the ground that it was quite impossible for him in that office to provide adequate instruction for medical students in the college. He was appointed instead director of medical studies and charged with the duty of working out a scheme of supervision for them. The implied corollary is that, for lectures and laboratory work, they would rely upon university provision.

Development was rapid thereafter. Supervisors in engineering and modern languages were appointed in 1904; by 1905 there were directors of studies in mathematics, moral science, theology, economics, natural sciences, history and law; and increasingly it became their duty to arrange for individual tuition. The college, too, came to expect its teaching officers to assume this particular duty: thus, when Benians was appointed a college lecturer in history in 1910, he was required, in addition to lecturing three times weekly, to take part in 'the college instruction by means of weekly essays'. Finally, in 1913, supervision arrangements were made for all natural scientists and mathematicians, though still at the option of the pupil. A good deal of discussion led up to this decision. The mathematical lecturers had reported in 1909 that most candidates for the mathematical tripos were now reading without coaches and that, therefore, 'individual college supervision... should be initiated to take the place of... the supervision for which men have usually gone to private tutors'. Three years later the committee investigating the position in the natural sciences declared roundly that, 'now that supervision is practically universal, a college without such a system is at a disadvantage'.

There is a footnote to this story of how college lecturers were becoming supervisors: the circumstances which brought about this transformation also helped to make anachronistic the one lecturer St John's maintained on the university's behalf—the Linacre lecturer in physic. This post, too, had been held by Dr D. MacAlister; and the opportunity was taken, when he vacated the lectureship in 1908 on his appointment as principal of Glasgow University, to convert it into an annual appointment 'of a man of mark in the medical profession to give a single public lecture in Cambridge'. The first of the new-model Linacre lectures was delivered in that same year by Professor William Osler, and took the very appropriate form of a review of 'the life and works of the founder'.[1]

We must return, however, to the main matter. Here the fact is that once again, as so often in the past, important changes in the pattern of college teaching were made during the pre-war generation without any comprehensive legislation. As college lecturing ceased to provide the main part of public instruction, college lecturers began to play a new role as the teachers of individuals and the college deliberately appointed staff with a view to providing this form of instruction. This was a policy which prepared the way for the modern accommodation between college and university and it was also one of the influences making the body of fellows more diverse. It included men who advanced the older studies: E. E. Sikes among

classical scholars; Sir Joseph Larmor, whose mathematical work comple-
mented that of Sir J. J. Thomson and contained elements Einstein later
developed; and H. F. Baker, 'who may fairly be said to have founded
a new school of geometry in Cambridge'.[1] A place was also found,
however, for men who were advancing new disciplines. St John's was
the college of J. R. Tanner, whose books on Tudor and Stuart history are
still current fare; of C. W. Previté-Orton, first professor of medieval
history at Cambridge; and of E. A. Benians, who did much to establish
a school of imperial and commonwealth studies. It was also the college of
William Bateson, one of the founders of the modern science of genetics; of
G. Udny Yule, who made an important contribution to the development
of statistical methods; and of W. H. R. Rivers, who did pioneering work
both as a psychologist and an anthropologist. The list might be made longer,
but something of the range of academic enquiry engaging the pre-war
fellows of the college is perhaps clear enough.

III

In aggregate the changes in the college's educational system had considerable significance—greater, indeed, than particular modifications of practice
immediately suggest. To some extent the same is true of other things.
Admittedly, there were no major alterations in the fabric of the college
after the erection, already recorded, of Penrose's building in chapel court.
Falling numbers, indeed, must have reduced the pressure upon accommodation save that, as the academic curriculum became more diversified,
there was sometimes difficulty in finding a home for college lectures.[2] On
the other hand, there were some improvements and some provision of
amenities. A public reading room (ancestor of the junior combination
room) was established in what is now part of the lower library in 1889 and
removed thence in 1902 to what is called today the Old Music Room. A
bicycle store was installed in first court in 1898 to relieve congestion in
rooms and on staircases; gas cooking replaced the old open fires in the
kitchen in 1885; the steward acquired an ice-pit on the playing fields in
1886; electric light was put into hall and chapel in 1892 and into the rest of

the college in 1911; the telephone reached the porter's lodge in 1901. In 1912 E. E. Sikes even raised with the council the desirability of the college building baths. The matter was deferred on grounds of expense, but a general meeting of fellows pressed the point and a committee was appointed to consider it in November 1913. War came next year, however, and deliberation ceased. In the event, the baths behind new court were not begun until 1921. Even then they lacked the blessing of Sir Joseph Larmor, though he regularly patronized them after they came into use, wearing as he crossed the court to reach them a mackintosh and cap in which he was never seen at any other time.[1]

In such a manner things now taken for granted were creeping in. Other changes, too, presaged modern ways. In 1900 the tutors were relieved of financial responsibility for their pupils, this charge being centralized in the hands of J. R. Tanner as tutorial bursar. Associated in part with this change was the establishment of a general college office, with a clerk to transact business not falling within the province of senior bursar or steward.[2] Change, however, was blended with a good deal which was old. Many fellows had gone rushing with 'rapturous rapidity into matrimony',[3] more of them than in the past were engaged in regular university and college teaching (a fact which may explain why a second fellows' table in hall was found necessary in 1892), and smoking was introduced into the small combination room in 1889—yet the marks of the older community of celibate clergymen gave way only slowly. Notice of vacant college livings was still given by the butler in hall until 1886 and provision was made for breakfast in the combination room, a repast at which some of the fellows entertained Oliver Wendell Holmes in that same year. In small things as well as great there was continuity as well as change.[4]

Much the same is true of undergraduate life. We are told that, in 1887, while the rational man breakfasted at 8.30, the fashionable one began the day with a sumptuous repast at 11.30—a reminder that the ways of the 1840's were not quite dead. The rules for discipline drawn up in 1907 inform us that paraffin was still used for lighting and that men were still expected to attend four chapels weekly (though the council in 1885 refused to make this compulsion absolute and in 1887 accepted Heitland's motion exempting those with conscientious scruples).[1] Those who did attend, however, might expect to find somewhat less hurried services than earlier in the century. The combined choir for Trinity and St John's had been given up in 1856, after Garrett became organist, and in 1889 an anonymous benefactor enabled the college to replace four of its eight lay clerks by choral students. The break with Trinity, moreover, also made it necessary for the college to establish its own school for its boy choristers and this was enlarged in 1915 when permission was given to the master of the school to take in additional boys.[2] In general, the effect of these changes was to make the choir more of a coherent unit and to give the chapel services more dignity than had been compatible with the older peripatetic arrangements.

Coming back to undergraduates, it might have been expected that a greater gulf would have been set between them and the fellows, many of whom were married and had domestic ties outside the college. Yet Bonney, looking back from the opening of the twentieth century upon a career which began in the mid-nineteenth, was convinced that the reverse was true. Without taking account of hospitality offered by senior to junior members, he discerned many new and intimate points of contact, particularly those afforded by the supervision system and by college societies.[3] The latter had become quite a feature of the college scene, with classical, natural sciences, historical and theological societies all in existence before 1914 and the debating society showing a remarkable capacity to survive occasional lean years. Sports clubs, too, called for a good deal of co-operation between dons and undergraduates, and a good deal of positive effort on the part of some of the fellows helped to bridge any gap there might have been. L. H. K. Bushe-Fox, as law lecturer, tutor from 1905 to 1916, and by the work he did for the Lady Margaret Boat Club and for the cricket and tennis clubs, was only one of those who joined 'the senior and junior members of St John's in a far closer understanding than hitherto'.[4] Something of the same results followed from two other events which were on the way to becoming institutions. The May week concert given by the musical society had more or less acquired that status by the 1880's, although Dr Garrett's mediation was required in 1887 to allay the council's alarm at a report that 'a professional lady singer' was to take part.[1] The May week ball came somewhat later, in the 1890's. It was held at first in the master's lodge, but soon moved to the hall and combination room. Not everyone, however, viewed this occasion with Dr Taylor's indulgence, for the council in 1895 felt that the tendency to make the ball an annual event was somewhat excessive. It was held, in consequence, rather inter-mittently down to 1914, when war suspended it along with many other curricular and extra-curricular activities in the college.

IV

This, however, was but one small effect of the First World War, which disrupted the life of the college to an extent to which the only possible parallel is the events of the few years around 1644. Numbers in residence began to fall from the Michaelmas term 1914 and that academic year ended 'without the colour and animation of May week, without races, concerts and balls...in the gloom of examinations whose importance it is hard to feel'. It was said that even the proctors complained of the desolation of the university. The Michaelmas term of 1915 opened with only ninety men in residence and by December, when the vice-chancellor's recruiting committee came to interview them, they were reduced to 74. In 1916 and 1917 the number of undergraduates was down to forty or less, and volun-tary bread rationing and then sugar rationing came in. College clubs and societies were in a state of suspension and, after earlier and more temporary military occupations, an officer cadet battalion took the places of under-graduates in new court. Many Johnians, of course, were absorbed into the forces and in the end some 150 of them, as well as two choristers and five college servants, did not return. Fellows as well as undergraduates and former members of the college were caught up in many forms of war service. A list would be out of place here, but it may be remembered that H. F. Russell Smith, friend of Rupert Brooke and one of those promising young historians the college bred in the immediate pre-war years, died of wounds in 1916; that T. R. Glover was released to go to India in 1915 to do work among soldiers for the Y.M.C.A.; and that Professor E. J. Rapson (already 53 in 1914), before departing for Cornwall as a full-time training officer, 'walked the four miles to Histon every Sunday morning to drill its volunteer company, returning in time to sing in the depleted choir of St John's College at 11 o'clock'.[1]

Clearly the interruption in the life of the college was drastic and perhaps it was inevitable that things could never be quite the same again, even if that could not be plainly discerned at the time. This is not to say that there was no thought for the future. Absent fellows and college officers were guaranteed reinstatement on their return; the college obtained powers to elect to open awards men prevented from competing at the normal time; the emoluments of scholars unable to complete their courses were held over; and reserve funds were created to meet the cost of these measures and to deal with repairs to the college buildings and on the college estates which had to be postponed in war-time. By February 1919 the council was able to envisage numbers returning to normality. Already there were 130 men in residence; 180 were expected in the Easter term and 250 at Michaelmas. That, however, proved to be only a beginning. The influx which the council anticipated did not cease when the old proportions were attained. In fact, the college has never again been so small as it was in 1914.[2]

The war years, then, separated a smaller from a larger college and they were very quickly followed by changes in the university at large which had important consequences for the colleges. Those changes, in many important respects, took account of tendencies already at work before 1914 and in particular of the progress made by intercollegiate or university provision in lecturing and examining. This progress was sometimes furthered by war-time shortages of staff and pupils, the reasons which moved the college to abandon a college for an intercollegiate examination in natural sciences in 1915.[3] An increase of university lecturers, however, was the crux of the matter. In 1918 the opinion of colleges was sought about the creation of a central fund maintained by tuition fees charged to students, the use of that fund to pay an enlarged staff of university lecturers and the desirability of colleges consulting university boards before they appointed college lecturers. Colleges, not unnaturally, saw in these proposals a threat to their independence, foresaw that they would be reduced 'to the level of boarding houses' and feared the rigidity of 'a great system of public lecturers'. Dr J. G. Leathem, bursar of St John's, played a leading part in formulating these forebodings and the most he would concede was expressed in his motion, which the college endorsed, that it was desirable that there should be voluntary co-operation by colleges to provide an improved scheme of intercollegiate or university lectures.[1]

There the matter rested until another royal commission was appointed to consider the whole situation of the university. At the same time, it ought not to be forgotten that, two years before the discussions of 1918, the college council had resolved that 'it is desirable to keep the college always closely in touch with the advancement of science, that there should be some fellows of the college engaged in university teaching and research, particularly in the natural sciences, to whom their fellowships would be assured on as secure a tenure as that of fellows who are college lecturers'.[2] For all its moment of intransigence in 1918, the college was being pushed by the logic of events into making itself a base for university teachers; and even before 1914 a new notion of the kind of teaching it would provide for its undergraduates was on the way to being established.

It is not always easy to discern with clarity all the tendencies at work in the college between 1881 and 1914, a difficulty which arises in part from the fact that these were years without commissions reforming the university or comprehensive legislation on the college's part. They were also years in which a good deal of an older world survived: college lecturing, private coaching and people. Dr Taylor himself was, in many ways, a master of the traditional sort and three successive presidents were men formed in much earlier generations. P. H. Mason (1882–1902) was elected a fellow in 1854, J. E. B. Mayor (1902–10) in 1849 and G. D. Liveing (1910–24) in 1853. We may not assume, of course, that such men were obstructive of all change: on the contrary, some of them had borne much of the responsibility for the great transformation which had taken place since 1850. On the other hand, not every proposal for continued change was welcomed by the elders of the college any more than by all of those who were much their juniors. When the time came for a new round of reforms in 1926, W. E. Heitland, critical as he had been of the defects of the college as he had first known it, was one who felt that change had now gone too far.[1]

For all that, the extent of the changes which did take place during the pre-war generation must not be underrated. The keynote is perhaps to be found in Dr Taylor's short way with visionary schemes and his cautious acceptance of proposals well thought out. Alterations, therefore, were apt to be pragmatic and piecemeal, but in aggregate they were important. Bushe-Foxe and Benians and Russell Smith were representative of a new type of fellow. The old coaches like Love and Webb were giving place to the new supervisor, whom MacAlister and Baker were making the characteristic college teacher. Intercollegiate arrangements were paving the way for 'a great system of public lecturers' and for the modern role of faculty and university. New standards were being set for undergraduates; a greater diversity of courses and wider prospects were available to them. All ages are ages of transition and this was no exception. The ultimate outcome was probably already inevitable in 1918, but the fact that it came so soon thereafter was also a result of the war itself. The four years which emptied the college transformed the external circumstances which played upon it, posed a new situation after those years were over and brought new men to the front to grapple with it. Their decisions in the decade after the armistice condition the character of the college in 1961, but they were not decisions made in a void. They were conditioned in turn by the reforms of the age of Bateson and by the way in which the implications of those reforms had been worked out in the times of Taylor and Scott.

VI

MODERN TIMES

VERY recent history, whether of a college or anything else, poses inevitable problems of perspective. It is all too easy, both for the observer and for those engaged in making them, to fail to discriminate between decisions of long and of short term significance, particularly in an era when changes are multifarious and momentous. The history of the modern college, therefore, is made all the more difficult to write by the fact that E. A. Benians could characterize the years between 1918 and 1940 as a period of change 'unexampled in the history of the university'. At the same time, he summarized the scale of the transformation which took place in the years between the wars in words we will do well to mark.

Never before [he said] had there been in the same time so rapid an increase in the number of teachers and students, in the facilities for research in the arts and sciences, or such multiplication of buildings by university and colleges. The decisive power and leadership restored to the university in 1926 after centuries of subordination was followed by activities impartially distributed around the whole circumference of academic knowledge....The colleges opened wide their doors to welcome a new stream of students.[1]

Benians, of course, spoke as vice-chancellor and of phenomena marking the history of the university in general; but what he said is relevant to the history of St John's College as much as it is to the history of any other part of the university. More than that, most of the tendencies he discerned at work between the wars were prolonged into the period after the Second World War. From that point of view, in fact, the war of 1939–45 appears to have been much less of a watershed than the war of 1914–18. The Second

World War, of course, like the first, obviously and even drastically affected the college. A high proportion of the fellows were called away into various forms of national service and at one point as many as thirty were absent at the same time. Again there was a military occupation of new court, this time by an R.A.F. training wing. Crops of onions and potatoes served for lawns in chapel court; and the number of junior members contracted, though far less dramatically than during the first war. Generally about two thirds of the normal complement were in residence, though for the time being many of them stayed only for a year.[1] When fellows and under-graduates returned, however, when airmen vanished and when grass grew where potatoes had been, the trends which reappeared were those already evident before 1939. The decisions of greatest moment for the modern college, in other words, were those taken between the wars, even though many implications and corollaries were only fully faced in the years after 1945.

Those who presided over this process of change were, in their different ways, not untypical of the transformation which was taking place. The gap between the pre-1914 and the post-1918 college was bridged by Sir Robert Scott, himself a new sort of master when compared with those who went before him. He was succeeded by E. A. Benians (1933–52), who entered the college as its first history scholar (an experiment, he told us, 'regarded rather doubtfully by the older men').[2] His mastership covered the period during which the changes of the 1920's came fully into operation, the interruption of the Second World War and the time of readjustment after it; and even before he became master, as tutor and senior tutor, he had borne a large responsibility for the manner in which the college adapted itself to the changed situation after 1918 and to the new relationship established in 1926 between the colleges and the university. Benians's successor was Sir James Wordie (1952–9), in whom for the first time the college had a scientist as master. The correlation between new men and new circumstances is almost too neat; but the new circumstances, at least, are matters of fact.

VII. ERNEST ALFRED BENIANS, MASTER 1933–1952

I

Among those circumstances the easiest to measure is the growing size of the college. The anticipation in 1919 that the number of undergraduates would build up rapidly was realized and exceeded. In both 1920 and 1930 the number of freshmen stood at around 140 and throughout the 1930's there were about 450 junior members in residence, compared with 274 in 1913. This upward trend continued after the interruption caused by the Second World War. The number of junior members reached a first peak of about 650 in 1949 and, after falling to around 575, crept up again to nearly 720 at the end of the 1950's. This last figure was in part a product of special circumstances, for the running down of national service brought in, at one and the same time, an influx of men who had completed their service and of others direct from school. None the less, the implication of the figures would seem to be that even the pre-1939 norms, to say nothing of those which prevailed before 1914, ceased to be adequate after 1945.[1]

This growth of St John's College before and after the Second World War was in no way peculiar to it. It was part of a great expansion of the university population in the country as a whole, mainly made possible by greatly increased assistance to students from public funds. Increased assistance, in turn, was consequent upon a growing awareness that modern society required an expanding supply of university graduates to satisfy its needs. The decision as to how open its gates should be to a new stream of students, however, was one made by the college itself. It was a decision which was anything but easy to make, for pressure for entry had to be balanced against the limits imposed by educational efficiency and the coherence of the college as a community. In the event the expansion of numbers was progressive and the series of decisions which brought that about may be accounted one of the specific contributions made by the college to the needs of modern society.

It was necessary, however, to do more than increase numbers. Facilities had also to be provided for men engaged in studies which assumed increased importance or appeared for the first time in the university curriculum. The most notable feature of the years after 1918 was an increase in the number of undergraduates studying scientific or technological subjects. Two fifths of the men who came up in 1952, compared with one fifth of those who came up in 1909, were engaged in honours courses in that general field; and a number of other men read engineering and agriculture for the ordinary B.A. degree. The increase in honours candidates in mechanical science was particularly striking, while veterinary medicine and chemical engineering were added after 1945 to the range of studies available. A smaller proportion of undergraduates (though a larger total in view of the increased numbers in the college) read mathematics and classics in 1952 than had been the case in 1909; law and history substantially increased their appeal; and a tenth of the freshmen of 1952 took honours courses, not available in 1909, in music, English, geography, archaeology and anthropology. The college deliberately encouraged this enlarged range of academic studies by extending to candidates in music, English and geography the open awards it offered to schoolboys. It also persisted in the pre–1914 endeavour to reduce the margin of men reading for ordinary degrees, with the result that an assumption that the great majority of men coming up will read for honours courses has become increasingly exclusive. Finally, those who achieve no degree at all have been reduced to insignificant numbers, explicable by illness or by those occasional errors from which no system of admissions can be quite immune.

Most, but not all, of the junior members of the college are undergraduates; but the rest of them also deserve a word. In the year 1959–60, leaving aside a certain number of graduates doing advanced courses of one sort or another, rather more than one in every ten junior members was a research student (the total was seventy-five). This total of research students, of course, has fluctuated somewhat from year to year; but the general trend has been fairly steadily upwards. Many have been men who pursued their undergraduate studies within the college, but many have also come from other places in Britain and elsewhere. In the Michaelmas Term of 1960, for example, nineteen research students entered the college from other universities—eight from the British Isles, eight from the commonwealth (Australia, Canada and South Africa), two from the United States of America and one from South America. The number of research students from outside has varied in different years and other countries than these have been represented; but the spread of 1960 is not untypical of recent years.

Like the increase in total numbers, the increase in the number of research students was a matter of deliberate policy. This question was already receiving attention in 1919. It was felt at that time that there was a need for more studentships and, in particular, for studentships which would be (unlike the older foundations) unrestricted as to subject. It was decided, therefore, to use for the assistance of research students the income from benefactions totalling £22,000 made to the college by Lord Strathcona and Mount Royal. It was provided that these studentships might be awarded to candidates in any subject and, in certain circumstances, to candidates other than members of the college.[1] In 1921 part of a bequest made by Philip Baylis (B.A. 1872) was similarly allotted to provide a studentship fund for mathematical science;[2] and in 1926 the college was offering for competition two Baylis, two Hutchinson, a Naden, a Slater and three Strathcona studentships, with a few smaller awards, to a total value of about £1600.[3] Since that date, it is true, a growing proportion of research students have been supported or mainly supported from public funds; but the initial determination to increase this element in the college was a matter of the college's own volition, before public provision on an expanding scale made that increase still more rapid.

The common factor in all these tendencies of the post-1918 era was a process of adjustment to a changing social situation. Industry and commerce, the public services and the professions have all required more trained men and men better trained. That pressure, in the last resort, operated directly or indirectly to expand the size of the college, to impose more rigorous standards, and to call for hospitality to men engaged in new disciplines, shifts in emphasis between old disciplines and the provision of facilities for post-graduate study aimed at advancing the frontiers of knowledge. This meant, on the one hand, that more men than in the past were engaged (whether as undergraduates or as research students) in scientific or technological studies; but the older and newer arts subjects, too, have seen their provinces expand. In the college, as well as in the university, the trend since 1918 has been, as Benians put it, for 'activities impartially distributed around the whole circumference of academic knowledge'.

II

These developments, in turn, created their own problems. To begin with, a community which grew from around 270 in 1914 to 720 in the 1950's needed more living space, public rooms, library facilities, dining and kitchen accommodation and so forth. Further, more undergraduates called for more college teachers requiring college rooms; and a measure of re-planning in the centre of Cambridge swept away many of the old lodging houses. A need for new buildings, therefore, very soon became evident and urgent, although it was not until 1938 that it became possible to begin the work of satisfying it on any substantial scale. In the years 1938–40, however, the modern parts of chapel court, north court and the service building to the north of the chapel were constructed after Sir Edward Maufe's design.[1] Not everyone has accepted the service building, in particular, as a satisfactory architectural solution to the problems offered by its site; but in chapel court, at least, the new buildings successfully unified the discordant elements which already existed there.

These new buildings provided the college with a sick-bay, a new porter's lodge, additional baths, a bicycle store and garage accommodation, and also with about sixty additional sets of rooms. Even in 1938, however, it was foreseen that north and chapel courts might be only the first stage of a larger plan to increase accommodation in college. The Second World War put any such provision out of the question for the time being, but its aftermath revived the crisis of accommodation in an even more acute form. The number of undergraduates in residence was always above the pre-1939 level and often substantially above it. Men in lodgings, in consequence, were more widely scattered over the face of Cambridge than ever before; there was little or no room in college for graduates or research students; men shared sets for the first time since the eighteenth century; three halls had to be instituted in place of the old one or two; and many fellows could expect no more than a single room, though this hardship, it ought to be said, was mitigated by the high incidence of matrimony.

The difficulty of finding a solution for this congestion was aggravated by high building costs and, as had been the case before 1939, by the heavy charge of maintaining and repairing older buildings. Even the comparatively modern chapel required substantial expenditure on its roof and windows. The ravages of death-watch beetle called for urgent work on the library roof in 1927–30. Wholesale repair, involving extensive demolition and reconstruction, was carried out in the first court in the 1930's; and similar operations began on a large scale in second court in 1958, are still proceeding and must extend eventually into third court. Old trees on the Backs, too, reached the end of their life and Dr Thomas Sharp was called in to advise the college on a general review of the landscaped grounds beyond new court. In accordance with his plan, the grounds and playing fields were replanted in 1952 and a formal garden was laid out to the north of the broad walk leading to Queen's Road.[1]

Growing numbers, however, did more than call for expenditure upon buildings: in combination with the increased diversity of studies, they made new demands upon the college's educational provision. Developments in this respect were also governed by external conditions. A royal commission on Oxford and Cambridge Universities was appointed in 1919. It reported in 1922 in favour of transferring all public instruction (lecturing, laboratory courses and so forth) to university faculties, the members of which would be based upon the colleges through the medium of reserving to university teaching officers a proportion of college fellowships. The implications of this report were worked out in the years 1923–5 by a statutory commission under Lord Ullswater and new university statutes came into operation in October 1926. These statutes, which implemented the recommendations of 1922, were a basis for the extensive and consequential revision of the college statutes which likewise took effect in 1926. The consequences of university reform were most clearly evident in the statutes governing fellowships. They laid down three main categories of fellows. Half those under title B were to be university officers, the remainder being holders of college teaching or other posts. At least seven fellowships (under title C) were to be reserved for professors or holders of certain other university posts. Finally, fellowships under title A involved an obligation on the part of their holders 'to devote themselves to the advancement of learning and research' and were normally to be tenable only for a period of three years. This last category recognized the increasing orientation of the modern university towards research and advanced study; and fellowships under titles B and C sought to realize the intention of the commissioners of 1922 to base the new and expanded body of university teachers in the collegiate communities.

In general, the 1926 statutes strengthened the connection between the college and the university by making members of university faculties and departments a substantial part of the college's fellowship. Powell's old ideal of collegiate autonomy which, in an attenuated form, Leathem had still been defending in 1918 had reached its term; and the trend for supervision to become the distinctive educational contribution of the colleges was likewise completed. None of this was absolutely new, but the completeness and comprehensiveness of the changes in 1926 made them radical. For that reason, if for no other, there were dissenting voices. The fears of 1918, that the colleges would be reduced merely to boarding houses, were still in the air; and T. R. Glover estimated that the new dispensation represented 'the triumph of practical efficiency over humanism and the substitution of science for culture'.[1] A somewhat longer view might suggest that these prognostications were excessively pessimistic. The arrangements which came into force in 1926 were more efficient, but that does not by itself discredit them. They were indispensable to exploit the new dimensions of scientific study, as the college had already recognized by closing its laboratories. They did not involve losing the intimacy of college teaching: from some points of view this was better secured by the supervision system than by the old régime of college lectures. Finally, a community of undergraduates engaged in many different studies, living together and adding to each other's experience, is much more than a boarding house. Acceptance of the new character of college teaching, combined as it was with the retention of the old character of colleges as places in which undergraduates educate each other, was a better thing than clinging in new and changing times to a world which had passed.

The teaching provision which the college was called upon to make by the new university and college statutes was scarcely less expensive of man-power than under the old dispensation; and more undergraduates and a greater diversity of studies made it more so. The consequence was that senior as well as junior members became more numerous. In 1927 there were forty-eight fellows, twenty-one of them holding under title B and providing the permanent nucleus of the college's teaching staff.[1] The corre-sponding figures today are rather more than seventy fellows with over forty holding under title B. Pressure in this direction was already being felt in the years immediately after the First World War, when a director of studies in agriculture, a supervisor in English, a college lecturer in music and a director of studies in geography were successively appointed;[2] and newer subjects still, like archaeology and biochemistry, were sub-sequently recognized by the creation for them of college teaching posts. While new studies called for new offices, so did expansion in older subjects. In October 1919, for example, with ninety men reading chemistry, a third supervisor in that subject was deemed necessary.[3] This process has continued and has created a new problem: the need for more supervisors than can be, at any given moment, provided from the body of fellows. It has been a necessary (if not a final) compromise to recognize, by such dining or other privileges which the college can confer, the services of those who, without being fellows, are part of the college's teaching staff.

More undergraduates, more fellows, the provision of new buildings and the maintenance of old have all helped to generate financial problems, and these have been exacerbated by economic change and by the long-term trend for the value of money to fall. In the face of these circumstances, indeed, some responsibilities could scarcely have been shouldered without extraneous help. To quote merely two examples: in 1953 the college undertook to offer scholarships and studentships to some medical students while in residence or during their subsequent clinical studies; and in 1958, as already pointed out, extensively to repair second and third courts. The first commitment was made possible by a substantial benefaction from Sir Humphry Davy Rolleston, who graduated from St John's in 1886 and became later an honorary fellow; the second could hardly have been contemplated without confident expectation, soon shown not to have been misplaced, of assistance from the Historic Buildings Fund, the Pilgrim Trust and, above all, from old members of the college. Generosity after this manner, in fact, has been of signal importance in modern times, as it has been throughout the college's history. Ours, in the words of E. A. Benians, 'is indeed a house built and adorned by many hands' and one which is enabled to do its work as a place of education by the munificence of benefactors of past times and the present time. A high proportion, moreover, of those who have raised the college's fabric and sustained its operations are, and always have been, its old members—a reminder that the denizens at any given moment are merely a part of the larger community of Johnians.

While benefactions solved some problems otherwise insoluble, it was also necessary to expand the regular revenue of the college. St John's remained and remains a substantial landowner, but the policy which R. F. Scott inaugurated as senior bursar was further developed by his successors in that office. Some property was sold and other property bought with the object of concentrating the college's holdings in high quality land which could be managed with convenience. A dividend was reaped from this policy, particularly in the good years for farming after 1939; but, while revenue from farm rents increased markedly, the proportion of the college's income drawn from this source declined. This was consequent upon a substantial increase in income from securities, particularly in the 1920's and the 1950's, and from properties (especially industrial properties) let on repairing leases, mainly after 1945. The investments which sustain the college, in short, were much more widely spread.

That fact, in turn, called for much more flexibility of financial management than in the old days when agricultural rents were virtually the only source of the college's income. In consequence, a great deal more had to be asked of senior bursars, and it was necessary to provide them with a larger office staff and with up-to-date office equipment. That is merely one manifestation of pressures which have altered much of the pattern of college administration. New channels of communication had to be kept open between the college and the university and between undergraduates, the many authorities which aid them and a great diversity of prospective employers. The two or three tutors of former times had given place, by the 1950's, to eight or nine, to cope with more applicants for admission, more pupils and the modern proliferation of 'forms'; and the office of senior tutor, with E. A. Benians as first incumbent, was formally instituted in 1926 to co-ordinate this branch of the college's affairs.[1] It was agreed, at the same time, to provide more clerical assistance for the tutors and similar enlargement of every departmental staff became necessary to handle a growing volume of business.

One result has been an enlargement of the circle of those who bear the old and honourable title of college servants. They were from the beginning part of the complement of the college and have their place, in small numbers it is true, in Fisher's statutes. Since that time their contribution to the corporate life of the college has been inestimable and the value of their service did not diminish with the increase of their numbers. Not even the bald record of a council minute can conceal the many facets of collegiate life which came under the influence of E. W. Lockhart. 'Mr Lockhart entered the service of the college in May 1886 and will have been in its service as library clerk, tutor's clerk, chief clerk and college butler for more than fifty years in all on 30 September 1936, and the council, in accepting with regret his resignation of the offices of chief clerk and college butler,...record their appreciation of his devoted and valuable services to the college.'[2] In token of that appreciation, the occasion of his retirement was marked by the presentation to him of a set of six silver stoups, the money for which was raised by personal subscription on the part of the fellows.

If the duration and variety of Lockhart's contribution to college life were remarkable, a good number of others also left their mark upon it. Sometimes there was more awe of J. H. Palmer, head porter from 1911 to 1936, than there was of deans, and more bibliographical help to be got in the college library from C. C. Scott than from supervisors. W. E. Wolfe, who retired in 1955 after forty-one years of service in the bursary, was a sage counsellor to others than bursars; and to watch him in converse with college tenants was an education in the art of public relations. L. Baker, too, was a friend to generations of sportsmen even though he produced wickets which made bowlers despair; and, when we think of those things which have made the reputation of the college, it ought not to be forgotten that R. E. Thoday, head gardener from 1928 to 1960, established in strange places its renown as a grower of Cox's orange pippins.

III

The foregoing modern developments are all of them reasonably tangible, but there were others the significance of which is much more difficult to assess. What weight ought to be placed, for example, upon the final abolition of compulsory chapel in 1919?[1] That decision, from one point of view, terminated something originally essential to collegiate life and rejected finally the exclusive Anglicanism which had dominated it for so long. On the other hand, the way had been prepared for this step by Victorian legislation and by the moderation with which the college had enforced its own rules well before 1914; and there may, in any case, have been an almost inverse relationship between the quality of the religious life which the chapel mirrored and the intensity of conscription. At least it can be said that the abolition of compulsion did not preclude new developments in the chapel music. Choral students completely replaced the old singing men; the organ was again extensively refashioned after 1945, making it one of the notable instruments in England; and the choir school became a preparatory school with some boarding accommodation, thus greatly extending its former local range of recruitment. These measures further improved the coherence and raised the quality of the choir, and helped to establish for the chapel music of St John's a reputation which formerly had belonged uniquely to the music of King's College.

Other changes are, even more, matters of subjective judgement. It may be felt, however, that circumstances and educational changes have continued to operate to bring closer the junior and senior members of the college, though in this process the part played by individuals is hard to overstress. If Bushe-Fox can stand for those who, before 1918, did much to this end, the same is true after that date of M. P. Charlesworth. Coming to St John's from Jesus College in 1922, he soon established himself as an outstanding classical scholar and teacher; but if he was admirable in that respect, 'his social gifts were unique and generously displayed'. As tutor from 1925 to 1937 and president from 1937 to 1950, he was a friend to more men and more diverse men than it might seem possible for one man to be. The service he gave, with such generosity and enthusiasm, was all the more valuable because the composition of the college was changing. The availability of public funds to assist undergraduates increased greatly after 1918 and particularly after 1945. It was, therefore, within the college's power still further to broaden its range of recruitment and to make itself still more representative of the whole community (though it ought not to be forgotten that, for much of its history and in accordance with Fisher's injunction, few colleges have done more for the poor man).[1] Some indication of its response may be found in the fact that, in the years 1934–8, 505 men came up from 204 different schools, in 1947–51 930 men from 330 schools and 1952–6 765 men from 311 schools. All in all, in the three quinquennia, 527 schools sent men to the college—161 of them 'public schools' (in the sense that they were represented at the Headmasters' Conference) and 366 others. While the former category of schools sent more men more regularly, the total range was still very wide.[2]

It may also be true that the greater accessibility of the college to all classes, combined with the assumption that virtually all undergraduates will read for honours, tended to erase the old lines of division between its members: those of a social character which impressed Samuel Butler and Heitland and those between sporting men and reading men which possibly assumed some importance at the end of the nineteenth century. The latter distinction could persist less easily when Cygnets and Willows offered facilities to rugby players and cricketers of less skill than enthusiasm, or when the Lady Margaret Boat Club added rugby, gentlemen's, medical and even B.A.'s boats to the growing number of crews it put upon the river. There is, perhaps, a similar explanation, along with the effects of two world wars and full employment, for a tendency towards plainer living for all and not only for those who could not afford to live better. The undergraduate of 1960 can look for less service than his predecessors expected. He cleans his own shoes; there is no lunchtime or evening visit from gyp or bedmaker; and some lines in the *Eagle* in 1954 are perhaps to be taken as indication that he eats less amply:

> Today we have tightening of belts. Spaghetti
> Glistens like coral in all of the neighbouring restaurants,
> And today we have tightening of belts.
> This is the large silver fork. And this
> Is the small steel knife, whose use you will see
> When you are given your meat. And this is the large helping,
> Which in your case you have not got.

The modern changes of this kind require time before we can appreciate their permanence, significance and ultimate direction; but, for all that, change in the decades after 1918 can hardly be called insubstantial. Studies, undergraduates and fellows became more diverse than ever; the education provided by the college was more closely related to the needs of an industrial and regulated society; and the university assumed much of the educational responsibility which, between Fisher's day and 1926, the college would have expected to bear. These changes, on the other hand, were not abrupt. Many of them began in Bateson's age or in the age which followed Bateson's; and they did not result in the college, regarded as a place 'knowing her children one by one',[1] abdicating all responsibility for teaching. On the contrary, it developed its own new provision, which supplemented that of the university and which had regard for the individual rather than the mass. Even the office of supervisor, however, had long roots. It grew out of the educational responsibility which Fisher imposed upon all fellows, of the tutor as Richard Holdsworth understood that office and of the private coach who, in the nineteenth century, made good some of the deficiencies of formal college teaching. Further, it has been all to the good that colleges have remained what from one point of view they always have been—boarding houses. It is a fruitful thing to bring together men of different backgrounds, interests and pre-occupations in a single community: for that is the means by which profit is drawn from 'unprofitable talk' and lessons are learned from 'trivial books'.

Change there was, then, in the twentieth century, even fundamental change: but that was not incompatible with significant continuity. In this there may be a certain inevitability, for a college is a community and its views about its purpose and about the way its purpose should be fulfilled must be, at any given moment, matters for joint decision by its members. In the nature of things some will not lose touch with the past and those with an eye to the future may not be lacking. If only for this reason change must be made to lie down with continuity, if only through the medium of compromise.

It was, however, the fortune of St John's that, for more than three decades after 1918, when change was both rapid and necessary, it enjoyed the services of E. A. Benians, first as its most influential tutor and then as its master. He has been described as a historian who valued the past, but whose faith was always in the future.[1] A faith in the future (and it was perhaps more—a vision of what the future ought to be) was an inestimable quality at a time when old landmarks were going; but that does not neces-sarily mean that the value he placed upon the past was less important. This was a matter of substance and not of form, of essence and not of accidents or manifestations. To use his own words, 'the forms of our existence change, the medium in which we work is different from age to age'; but 'the true treasure of the college is the original purpose of its foundation, made stronger or weaker by its fulfilment in each succeeding generation'.

What Benians meant by these phrases is important, for he made them influential. His conception of the original and continuing purpose of the college emerges most clearly from his reflections, scattered over much that he said and wrote, upon the life and deeds of John Fisher. Fisher, he considered, discerned that the university, in that age, needed new life and learning; but 'beyond the university he saw the needs of his time and how the university could help to supply them,...and he longed for men educated and moved to the service of their fellow men'. Fisher, in other words, was concerned for 'humane and fruitful knowledge' and for education as a 'means of service'. For that reason and in the circumstances of the early sixteenth century, he made St John's a school of practical theology. This unique purpose was soon outgrown, but what was essential in it did not therefore cease to be 'the true treasure of the college'. In the words of Benians once again, 'time, which has ripened the colour of our walls, has changed the character of our work, enlarged its range and multiplied its ends. Instead of breeding the incumbents of one or two professions, the colleges now prepare men for an ever widening circle of occupations, and the influence of collegiate education makes itself felt through all the texture of the national life'.[1] It is still, in fact, the part of the college to equip men with the means to serve, even though most of them will serve their fellow men very differently than Fisher's poor scholars did. It is in this way that we must interpret the faith displayed in the future and the value placed upon the past by E. A. Benians. There was no question of reverencing the past for its own sake: it was valued for the discipline and sense of direction which it brought to his faith in the future. That discipline and a sense of direction were vitally necessary at a time of rapid and fundamental changes; they provided guiding ideas which shaped and are still shaping today's college; and both his faith in the future and the value he placed upon the past will be needed when other changes come, as they must come, in days which still lie ahead.

BIBLIOGRAPHY

In the detailed notes which follow, reference is made to certain general works on the history of the college only when they are specifically quoted or when a particular point of view has been adopted on a matter which is controversial. It may be assumed, however, that the following works have been used throughout and that they frequently contain far greater detail on the matters discussed in the text.

I. GENERAL HISTORIES

(a) Of the University: the most recent account is that by J. P. C. Roach in *Victoria County History of Cambridgeshire and the Isle of Ely*, III (1959), where there are full references to sources and earlier works.

(b) Of the College:

T. Baker, *History of the College of St John the Evangelist, Cambridge*, ed. J. E. B. Mayor (1869). Baker's history occupies pp. 1–241 of this edition. It is referred to in the Notes as Baker–Mayor.

J. B. Mullinger, *St John's College* (1901).

R. F. Scott, *St John's College, Cambridge* (1907).

2. COLLEGE BUILDINGS

R. Willis and J. W. Clark, *Architectural History of the University of Cambridge*, II (1886), 233–350.

N. Pevsner, *The Buildings of England: Cambridgeshire* (Penguin Books, 1954), 120–32: a lively introductory account.

Inventory of the Historical Monuments in the City of Cambridge (1959), II, 187–202.

3. COLLEGE FINANCE

H. F. Howard, *An Account of the Finances of the College of St John the Evangelist in the University of Cambridge, 1511–1926* (1935).

The sources in print for the college's history include four main collections to which fairly full references have been given in the Notes. These are:

(1) The *Eagle*, which provides a term-by-term record of events since 1858 as well as many articles dealing with episodes in the history of the College, published documents and other source material.

(2) Most notable in this last category are the 'Notes from the College Records' contributed by R. F. Scott to almost every number of the *Eagle* from 1890 to 1915. Some copies of these 'Notes', with a certain amount of additional material,

were bound up into four substantial volumes which can be consulted in the college library.

(3) J. E. B. Mayor's edition of Baker's *History* contains some 870 pages of additional material, including Cole's continuation of Baker and almost everything else besides. Order is not a salient characteristic of the arrangement, but there is much in this glorious rag-bag to reward the unhurried reader.

(4) *Admissions to the College of St John the Evangelist in the University of Cambridge*, ed. J. E. B. Mayor and R. F. Scott, I–IV. In addition to a full transcript of the admissions registers from 1630 to 1802, vols. III and IV contain detailed biographies of a high proportion of members of the College from 1715 to 1802. To continue this work for earlier and later periods would be a useful contribution to English and college history.

NOTES

PAGE 1

1 Baker–Mayor (see p. 129), I, 68; *Documents relating to the University and Colleges of Cambridge* (1852), III, 230–44.

PAGE 2

1 For what follows see R. F. Scott, *Eagle*, XVI, 342–6; XIX, 1–3; XXVII, 1–27; XXXI, 283 and his paper privately published in 1918 and reprinted in his *Notes from the College Records*, IV, 203–50; *Collegium Divi Johannis Evangelistae*, 103 *sqq.* for the text of the Lady Margaret's will, also pp. 61–6; E. Miller, *Eagle*, LVII, 1–7; D. Hay, *Polydore Vergil*, 6; E. A. Benians, *John Fisher* (1935).

PAGE 5

1 *Early Statutes of the College of St John the Evangelist*, ed. J. E. B. Mayor, 48–9, 301–2; Baker–Mayor, I, 157–61.
2 *Ibid.* 95; the list of benefactors, with the nature and purpose of their benefactions, is most conveniently to be found in A. F. Torry, *Founders and Benefactors of St John's College, Cambridge* (1888).

PAGE 6

1 Baker–Mayor, I, 70–1; *Eagle*, XXXI, 147 *sqq.*

PAGE 7

1 For the original character of the grounds, see J. S. Boys Smith, *Eagle*, LIV, 300–1.

PAGE 8

1 *Early Statutes*, ed. Mayor, 166.
2 T. Fuller, *History of the University of Cambridge* (ed. J. Nichols, 1840), 168.
3 *Eagle*, XVI, 348.
4 Baker–Mayor, I, 86–7, 107; *Eagle*, XXXII, 4–9.
5 For what follows, see generally *Early Statutes*, ed. Mayor, *passim*; also R. F. Scott, *Notes from the College Records*, IV, 251 *sqq.* and G. C. Evans, *Eagle*, LVI, 196–200.

PAGE 9

1 Torry, *Founders and Benefactors*, 3, 5–6; *5th Report from the Select Committee on Education* (1818), Appx. B, 464 *sqq.*

PAGE 11

1 Conyers Read, *Mr Secretary Cecil and Queen Elizabeth* (1955), 27.

PAGE 12

1 *V.C.H. Cambs.* III, 167.
2 *Eagle*, XXXV, 34.
3 *D.N.B.* II, 150–9; *The Whole Works of Roger Ascham*, ed. J. A. Giles, I (Letters), 52.

PAGE 14

1 Baker–Mayor, I, 102, 456; J. Lewis, *Life of John Fisher* (1855), II, 356.
2 *V.C.H. Cambs.* III, 172–3.
3 *Works of R. Ascham*, ed. Giles, IV (*The Scholemaster*), 234–5.

PAGE 15

1 Baker–Mayor, I, 104–5; Fuller, *History of University of Cambridge*, 168.
2 *Works of R. Ascham*, ed. Giles, IV, 235.

PAGE 16

1 *V.C.H. Cambs.* III, 181.
2 *Works of R. Ascham*, ed. Giles, I (Letters), 138.
3 *Ibid.*; M. H. Curtis, *Oxford and Cambridge in Transition*, 51.

PAGE 17

1 R. F. Scott, *Notes from the College Records*, IV, 281.

PAGE 18

1 *Works of R. Ascham*, ed. Giles, I (Letters), 47–9, 53–6.
2 *Early Statutes*, ed. Mayor, 3–255.
3 Baker–Mayor, I, 130–3.
4 *Works of R. Ascham*, ed. Giles, IV (*The Scholemaster*), 235–6.

PAGE 19

1 Baker–Mayor, I, 148, 153–4; *Eagle*, XXVIII, 135.
2 Baker–Mayor, I, 162–3; II, 587–8; H. C. Porter, *Reformation and Reaction in Tudor Cambridge*, 119–35.

PAGE 20

1 Baker–Mayor, I, 166, 169, 173–6, 395; II, 590, 593, 596; *Eagle*, XXXV, 261–3; the Elizabethan statutes are printed in Appx. B of the *5th Report from the Select Committee on Education* (1818).
2 Curtis, *Oxford and Cambridge in Transition*, 207 *sqq.*

PAGE 21

1 Baker–Mayor, II, 599–602; *Eagle*, XXVIII, 1–23; XXXV, 263–300; Porter, *op. cit.* 183 *sqq.*
2 Baker–Mayor, I, 190; II, 606–9; *Eagle*, 160–1.
3 Porter, *op. cit.* 201–6; Baker–Mayor, I, 196.
4 *Ibid.* I, 203, 487–8; *Eagle*, XVI, 230 *sqq.*; XXIII, 295–302.
5 Baker–Mayor, I, 213–15, 502–3; II, 625–6.

PAGE 22

1 *Ibid.* I, 93, 217–18; II, 629–31; *Eagle*, XVII, 474; XXIV, 77–8, 153–5; XXVI, 5; LV, 104–1.
2 *Ibid.* XXXIV, 1–5.

PAGE 23

1 For these and the following events, see Baker–Mayor, I, 219–20, 225–6, 295–6, 538; II, 633–4, 639; *Eagle*, XXIV, 171–3; XXXIII, 257 *sqq.*; XXXIV, 159–61; LV, 141–2.
2 *Henry Newcome's Autobiography*, I (Chetham Soc., 1852), 7.

PAGE 24

1 *Eagle*, XXIV, 162–3; Baker–Mayor, II, 603.
2 *Eagle*, XXIX, 277 *sqq.*
3 J. A. Venn, *Entries of the Various Colleges in the University of Cambridge, 1544–1906*; C. H. Cooper, *Annals of Cambridge*, III, 554; *Admissions to the College of St John the Evangelist, Cambridge*, ed. J. E. B. Mayor and R. F. Scott, I (1630–65).

PAGE 26

1 *Eagle*, XVII, 1 *sqq.*, 142 *sqq.*, 343 *sqq.*; LIV, 226.
2 *Ibid.* IX, 371; XVII, 8.
3 A. F. Torry, *Founders and Benefactors*, 44–7; G. C. Evans, *Eagle*, LVI, 199–204.

PAGE 27

1 *Eagle*, LIV, 301–2.
2 Baker–Mayor, I, 415–16.
3 *Eagle*, XXIX, 25–6.

PAGE 28

1 Baker–Mayor, I, 195, 199, 448.
2 *Eagle*, XXXV, 264.

PAGE 29

1 Baker–Mayor, I, 374, 376, 380–1, 384, 388, 437.

PAGE 30

1 *Admissions*, ed. Mayor and Scott, I, 1–9.
2 The registers of fellows and seniors are printed in Baker–Mayor, I, 281 *sqq.*; and biographical details are to be found in J. and J. A. Venn, *Alumni Cantabrigiensis*.

PAGE 31

1 See, in general, M. H. Curtis, *Oxford and Cambridge in Transition*, 126 *sqq.*

PAGE 32

1 Arber's *English Reprints*, IV, 121; *Works of R. Ascham*, ed. Giles, I (Letters), 69; *Eagle*, L, 23–4.
2 *Tudor Economic Documents*, ed. R. H. Tawney and E. Power, I, 326.
3 *Eagle*, XVII, 92; Baker–Mayor, I, 183; G. I. Soden, *Geoffrey Goodman, Bishop of Gloucester*, 45 *sqq.*

PAGE 33

1 A. F. Torry, *Founders and Benefactors, passim*; Baker–Mayor, I, 150, 371–2, 405–13, 419–20, 447; *Eagle*, XVIII, 1 *sqq.*; XIX, 309 *sqq.*; XX, 487 *sqq.*
2 *Eagle*, XIX, 541–2; XXI, 153–4; XXVII, 319–26.

PAGE 34

1 *Ibid.* XIX, 538 *sqq.*; XXI, 153 *sqq.*; XXIII, 18–19; XXVII, 319 *sqq.*; Baker–Mayor, I, 477–81, 484, 496–7, 528–9.

PAGE 35

1 Arber's *English Reprints*, IV, 121–2.
2 *Eagle*, XIII, 2.
3 *Ibid.* XVI, 148–50; XVII, 92; XXXVI, 145–52.

PAGE 36

1 *Ibid.* XIV, 253; XXX, 272–3; H. C. Porter, *Historical Journal*, III (1960), 199.

PAGE 37

1 *Eagle*, I, 156; XIV, 376–80; XXV, 268; XXIX, 151; XXXI, 25 *sqq.*; LIII, 164–70; Baker–Mayor, I, 121; II, 573–4.
2 *Ibid.* I, 532.

PAGE 38

1 Baker–Mayor, I, 544–5; *Eagle*, XVI, 141, 145; XXXIII, 261; R. F. Scott, *St John's College, Cambridge*, 50; *Life of Matthew Robinson*, ed. J. E. B. Mayor, 21–2.

PAGE 40

1 *Eagle*, IX, 372 *sqq.*; X, I *sqq.*; XVI, 142; XIX, 144–5, 529–31; Baker–Mayor, II, 646; *Life of Matthew Robinson*, 19.

2 There is a convenient summary in Curtis, *Oxford and Cambridge in Transition*, 108–13, 131–3; the original MS. is in the Library of Emmanuel College.

PAGE 43

1 Baker–Mayor, I, 233–4, 542.

2 *Ibid.* II, 658–9, 1036; *5th Report from Select Committee on Education* (1818), Appx. B, 472; *Eagle*, LV, 142.

PAGE 44

1 Baker–Mayor, I, 991, 993; *Diary of Abraham de la Pryme* (Surtees Society, 1869), 20.

PAGE 45

1 *Eagle*, XXIV, 309–12; Baker–Mayor, II, 993–4.

2 R. Masters, *Memoir of...Thomas Baker* (1784), 139–40.

3 *Cambridge under Queen Anne*, ed. J. E. B. Mayor, 18 *et passim*.

PAGE 46

1 Baker–Mayor, II, 1015–17.

2 *Ibid.* 1022–32; Conclusion Book, 1736–86, 43.

PAGE 47

1 *Ibid.* 144, 147, 155.

2 *Admissions*, ed. Mayor and Scott, I–III.

3 *Historical Monuments Commission: City of Cambridge*, II, 188; Baker–Mayor, I, 544.

PAGE 48

1 *Cambridge under Queen Anne*, ed. Mayor, 18, 34 *sqq.*

2 *Eagle*, XV, 469–74; XLVIII, 63–70; LIV, 294.

3 *Ibid.* LIV, 302–6; *The Journeys of Celia Fiennes*, ed. C. Morris, 65–6.

4 A. F. Torry, *Founders and Benefactors*, 39–41, 60–1, 66–7.

PAGE 49

1 Conclusion Book, 1736–86, 54, 63, 144, 164.

2 *Ibid.* 85, 105, 132.

3 *Ibid.* 57, 97.

PAGE 50

1 *Ibid.* 90, 93, 98; and for Powell's memorandum, *Eagle*, **xx**, 137 *sqq.*

PAGE 51

1 Torry, *op. cit.* pp. **vi**, 73–4; *Eagle*, **xxii**, 172–3.

2 The biographical material in what follows is drawn, where no other reference is given, from the text and appendix to *Admissions*, ed. Mayor and Scott, **iii**, and from the registers of fellows and seniors in Baker–Mayor, **i**, 281 *sqq.*

PAGE 52

1 Conclusion Book, 1736–86, 57.

PAGE 53

1 D. A. Winstanley, *Unreformed Cambridge*, 98.

2 *Eagle*, **xix**, 138–40; *D.N.B.* **xlvi**, 397–401; W. Osler, *Thomas Linacre*, 49–50.

PAGE 54

1 J. Mainwaring, *Sermons on Several Occasions* (1780), pp. lxxx–lxxxi; *Admissions*, **iii**, 478; *Boswell's Life of Johnson*, ed. G. B. Hill and L. F. Powell, **iii**, 248; **v**, 29, 88.

PAGE 55

1 W. Langdon-Brown, *Some Chapters in Cambridge Medical History*, 48 *sqq.*; St John's College MS. W 23; Conclusion Book, 1736–86, 161.

PAGE 56

1 *Eagle*, **xvii**, 258; *Cambridge under Queen Anne*, ed. Mayor, 21, 24, 33; Conclusion Book, 1736–86, 16, 151.

2 *Eagle*, **xvii**, 258; *Cambridge under Queen Anne*, ed. Mayor, 19, 21.

PAGE 57

1 *Eagle*, **xxvii**, 135.

2 St John's College MS. W 3 (James 358).

3 *Cambridge under Queen Anne*, ed. Mayor, 55–6.

4 E.g. *English History from Essex Sources*, ed. A. F. J. Brown, 132.

PAGE 61

1 *Admissions*, ed. Mayor and Scott, **ii–iii**.

2 *Eagle*, **xvii**, 246 *sqq.*; *Cambridge under Queen Anne*, ed. Mayor, 19 *sqq.*; *Diary of Abraham de la Pryme*, 32.

3 *V.C.H. Cambs.* **iii**, 226–33; Winstanley, *Unreformed Cambridge*, 39 *sqq.*

PAGE 62

1 The mathematical honours lists from 1748 are in *Historical Register of the University of Cambridge...to the year 1910*, 443 *sqq.*; H. Gunning, *Reminiscences of Cambridge*, I, 89.
2 *Cambridge under Queen Anne*, ed. Mayor, 55–6.
3 J. Mainwaring, *Sermons on Several Occasions*, pp. lxix–lxx.
4 J. B. Mullinger, *St John's College*, 226.

PAGE 63

1 *Cambridge under Queen Anne*, ed. Mayor, 34, 53–4, 65; *Diary of Abraham de la Pryme*, 20, 22–5; G. Pryme, *Autobiographic Recollections*, 4–5.
2 *Diary of Abraham de la Pryme*, 19–20; *Eagle*, XVII, 256–7; XXIV, 173.

PAGE 64

1 *V.C.H. Cambs.* III, 235.

PAGE 66

1 Winstanley, *Cambridge in the Eighteenth Century*, 240 *sqq.*; *Unreformed Cambridge*, 100–1.
2 E. A. Benians, *Eagle*, LIV, 102–4; Baker–Mayor, II, 1055, 1071; Conclusion Book, 1736–86, 168.
3 Baker–Mayor, II, 1071–3; *Eagle*, VII, 334–7; W. Ludlam, *Astronomical Observations made in St John's College, Cambridge, in the years 1767 and 1768: with an Account of Several Astronomical Instruments*.
4 Baker–Mayor, II, 1055.
5 *Ibid.* 1069.

PAGE 67

1 *Eagle*, LIV, 305–6.

PAGE 68

1 *Ibid.* IX, 278–9; Baker–Mayor, II, 1058–9, 1067–8.
2 *Ibid.* 1079–82.

PAGE 69

1 *Ibid.* 1089–92; St John's College MS. K 42 (James 351); Conclusion Book 1736–86, 272, 275; 1786–1846, 52; *Admissions*, ed. Mayor and Scott, IV, 376–9; *Eagle*, XXXIV, 94–8.
2 Conclusion Book, 1786–1846, 59–64, 93; *Eagle*, XXII, 145 *sqq.*

PAGE 70

1 H. M. Hyde, *Rise of Castlereagh*, 45 *sqq.*; R. I. and S. Wilberforce, *Life of William Wilberforce*, I, 10–12; C. Tennyson, *Alfred Tennyson*, 6; E. A. Benians, *Eagle*, LIV, 74–82; Mary Moorman, *William Wordsworth*, 90; B. R. Schneider, *Wordsworth's Cambridge Education*, 5–7.

PAGE 71

1 *Admissions*, ed. Mayor and Scott, IV.

PAGE 72

1 J. A. Venn, *Entries of the Various Colleges*; *Graham Commission Report*, 145.

PAGE 73

1 Baker–Mayor, II, 1094–9; *Eagle*, XVI, 399.
2 Winstanley, *Early Victorian Cambridge*, 24–6; *Eagle*, XXXI, 156–7.

PAGE 74

1 Baker–Mayor, II, 1095, 1098–9; *Eagle*, LV, 143; LVIII, 30 *sqq.*; Conclusion Book, 1786–1846, 10 July 1819.
2 *Eagle*, XVII, 92; XIX, 597.

PAGE 75

1 *Ibid.* XXI, 1 *sqq.*; Conclusion Book, 1786–1846, 8 April 1837.
2 *Ibid.* 22 April 1837.
3 The disadvantages had been recognized as early as 1588, and a petition to amend this part of the statutes had been contemplated in 1766: *Eagle*, XXXV, 272; Conclusion Book, 1736–86, 176.
4 G. M. Trevelyan, *Trinity College*, 78; *Admissions*, ed. Mayor and Scott, IV, 340–1.

PAGE 76

1 *Eagle*, XX, 625 *sqq.*; XXII, 145–7.
2 N. Pevsner, *The Buildings of England: Cambridgeshire*, 127–8; *Eagle*, LV, 169; *Poems, Letters and Prose Fragments of Kirke White*, ed. J. Drinkwater, 204.
3 J. S. Boys Smith, *Eagle*, LVI, 185–93.

PAGE 77

1 J. S. Boys Smith, *Eagle*, LIII, 147–61; LIV, 307–10.
2 *Eagle*, XX, 512 *sqq.*; XXV, 49 *sqq.*
3 C. A. Bristed, *Five Years in an English University* (1852), 143.

PAGE 78

1 Winstanley, *Early Victorian Cambridge*, 160–6, 177–8; A. J. Berry, *A Sketch of the Study of Crystallography and Mineralogy in Cambridge, 1808–1931*; W. Langdon-Brown, *Cambridge Medical History*, 76–7; Eagle, XI, 293–302; XIX, 62 *sqq.*; *Autobiography of Charles Darwin* (ed. of 1929), 26–8, 34; J. W. Judd, *The Coming of Evolution*, 97–9.

2 *Eagle*, XLVI, 150.

PAGE 79

1 *Ibid.* XVII, 135–6; XVIII, 306, 603; XXXVI, 198.

2 *Ibid.* XVIII, 183 *sqq.*; T. R. Glover, *Cambridge Retrospect*, 88–9.

3 *Eagle*, XXX, 300–1; XLVI, 134 *sqq.*, 187 *sqq.*

PAGE 80

1 Admissions Register, 1835–84.

2 *Eagle*, XXX, 295.

3 *V.C.H. Cambs.* III, 441; *Poems, Letters and Prose Fragments of Kirke White*, ed. Drinkwater, 204.

4 *Eagle*, XXX, 295; XXXI, 189–90.

PAGE 81

1 In *The Way of All Flesh*; cf. H. Festing Jones, *Samuel Butler*, I, 45 *sqq.*

2 *Eagle*, XVIII, 135–6.

3 *Ibid.* IX, 270; XXV, 52; Conclusion Book, 1736–86, 295.

PAGE 82

1 *Eagle*, XXV, 49 *sqq.*; XXXI, 185–6.

2 *Ibid.* XXIII, 107.

3 *Ibid.* XI, 295; Conclusion Book, 1846–72, 7 June 1852.

4 *Eagle*, XX, 442–4; XXIX, 341–3; XXXII, 191.

PAGE 83

1 *Ibid.* XI, 458–78.

PAGE 84

1 *Ibid.* XXI, 13–23.

2 *Statuta Collegii Divi Johannis Evangelistae Cantabrigie* (1849).

3 In general see J. E. B. Mayor's and H. J. Roby's recollections, *Eagle*, XXXI, 189–209.

4 Conclusion Book, 1846–72, 8 July 1853.

PAGE 85

1 *Ibid.* 17 October 1853; *Eagle*, XX, 716; XLII, 163.

2 H. J. Roby, *To the Master and Fellows of St John's College, Cambridge: Of the Government and Tuition* (1857).

3 W. E. Heitland, *After Many Years*, 141 *sqq.*

PAGE 86

1 *The Statutes of the College of St John the Evangelist in the University of Cambridge* (1857–61); *Eagle*, XXXI, 195 *sqq.*

2 Conclusion Book, 1846–72, 25 April 1860; 17 March 1860; 17 June 1867; *Eagle*, XI, 349–50.

3 *Eagle*, VI, 73; VIII, 369; XI, 48–51.

4 Conclusion Book, 1865–88, 4 June 1874.

PAGE 87

1 College appointments are recorded in the Conclusion Books and details of triposes in *Historical Register of the University of Cambridge...to...1910*.

2 The list is in *Eagle*, X, 120–1, 247.

3 W. E. Heitland, *After Many Years*, 125.

4 *Eagle*, XLIX, 187–92.

PAGE 88

1 *Eagle*, XXIII, 349–50; XXXVII, 141–2; N. G. Annan, *Leslie Stephen*, 26–7.

2 Heitland, *After Many Years*, 124 *sqq.*; *Eagle*, XXIII, 82.

PAGE 89

1 Conclusion Book, 1865–88, 27 May 1878; *Eagle*, VIII, 254.

2 *Ibid.* XVII, 654 *sqq.*; XLIII, 263; Heitland, *op. cit.* 176.

PAGE 90

1 *Statutes for the College of St John the Evangelist in the University of Cambridge* (1885).

PAGE 91

1 *Eagle*, IX, 315; XLIV, 98; T. G. Bonney, *Memories of a Long Life*, 56.

PAGE 92

1 *Eagle*, LV, 144–5; LVIII, 17–29; Council Minute, 188/10; N. Pevsner, *The Buildings of England: Cambridgeshire*, 129–30.

2 *Eagle*, X, 194–5.

3 Heitland, *op. cit.* 106–8.

4 Admissions Register, 1835–84.

PAGE 93

1 St John's College MS. U 22; *Eagle*, XX, 659–60; XXI, 368–70; *Cambridge History of the British Empire*, VII (2), 36, 56, 132–4.

2 *Eagle*, XXII, 81 *sqq.*; 237–44; XXXIV, 109–11; XXXVI, 197 *sqq.*; XLVI, 171 *sqq.*

3 *Graham Commission Report*, 145; *Eagle*, XI, 57, 355.

4 Conclusion Book, 1865–88, 9 May 1876.

PAGE 94

1 Heitland, *op. cit.* 118–19.

2 *Eagle*, LIV, 311–12.

3 *Ibid.* VI, 256.

4 *Ibid.* XI, 470.

PAGE 95

1 St John's College MS. U 22.

2 *Eagle*, XXX, 64 *sqq.*

PAGE 96

1 *Ibid.* XLVIII, 3 *sqq.*

2 *Ibid.* XXIII, 82.

3 Council Minutes, 7 December 1883 and 24 October 1884; Conclusion Book, 1888–97, *passim.*

PAGE 97

1 Council Minutes, 438/8, 440/7.

2 *After Many Years*, 228.

PAGE 98

1 J. A. Venn, *Entries of the Various Colleges*; C. W. Guillebaud, *Eagle*, LVI, 123–4.

2 Council Minute, 391/7.

3 *Ibid.* 261/13.

PAGE 99

1 *Eagle*, XII, 56; XXXIV, 122.

2 *Ibid.* XIV, 49.

3 *Ibid.* XIII, 225.

PAGE 100

1 E.g. Conclusion Book, 1865–88, 22 December 1884; Council Minutes, 27 February 1885 and 14 October 1887.

2 *Eagle*, XLVI, 190–1.

3 *Ibid.* XXIII, 96; Council Minutes, 741/10, 926/4.

PAGE 101

1 J. J. Thomson, *Recollections and Reflections*, 142.
2 Council Minute, 464/5.

PAGE 102

1 *Eagle*, XXI, 226–7, 242.

PAGE 103

1 Conclusion Book, 1865–88, 2 November 1883; *Eagle*, XV, 48–9, 265–6.
2 Conclusion Book, 1865–88, *passim*; Council Minute, 25 April 1884.
3 *Eagle*, LI, 277; Council Minutes, 153/22, 842/3.
4 *Ibid.* 173/2.
5 *Ibid.* 720/6.

PAGE 104

1 *Eagle*, XX, 744; XLIX, 272–3.
2 *Ibid.* LV, 12; Council Minute, 720/6.

PAGE 105

1 *Ibid.* 627/7, 696/7, 700/2, 721/4, 812/3, 844/5, 844/6, 892/10, 913/6; *Cambridge Review*, XXIX (1907–8), 357; W. Osler, *Thomas Linacre*, 3–4.

PAGE 106

1 *Eagle*, LII, 186–91; LVII, 80–3.
2 E.g. Council Minute, 285/3.

PAGE 107

1 *Eagle*, XV, 186–7, 519; XXIV, 393; LII, 187; Council Minutes, 146/9, 347/5, 501/3, 538/7, 574/11, 629/3, 861/4, 903/4, 925/7, 1116/18.
2 *Ibid.* 592/7, 593/6, 890/2, 896/12, 898/16.
3 *Cambridge University Reporter*, 1882–3, 767; and c.f. J. R. Tanner's remark recalled by T. R. Glover, *Cambridge Retrospect*, 105.
4 *Eagle*, XVI, 81; XXII, 172; Council Minutes, 146/7, 341/2.

PAGE 108

1 *Ibid.* 171/2, 772/8; *Eagle*, LV, 45–7.
2 Council Minutes, 223/17, 951/1.
3 *Eagle*, XXX, 309.
4 *Ibid.* XXXVII, 379 *sqq.*

PAGE 109

1   Council Minute, 180/7.

PAGE 110

1   *Ibid.* 952/2, 959/7, 968/10, 1070/5; *Eagle*, XXXVI, 329 *sqq.*; XXXVIII, 94–9, 206 *sqq.*;
    L, 255.
2   Council Minutes, 972/7, 1047/3; *Eagle*, XXVI, 332.
3   Council Minute, 957/4.

PAGE 111

1   *Ibid.* 1037/4, 1040/4.
2   *Ibid.* 979/13.

PAGE 112

1   *After Many Years,* 220.

PAGE 113

1   *Cambridge University Reporter,* 1940–1, 131 *sqq.*

PAGE 114

1   *Eagle,* LII, 306 *sqq.*
2   *Ibid.* LV, 12.

PAGE 115

1   *Ibid.* LVI, 123–4.

PAGE 117

1   *St John's College Regulations, Standing Orders, etc.,* 57, 64.
2   *Statutes for the College of St John the Evangelist* (1927), 131. The use of this fund
    subsequently reverted to what would appear to have been the original intention:
    the provision of scholarships for undergraduates.
3   Council Minute, 1236/4.

PAGE 118

1   *Eagle,* L, 253 *sqq.*; LIII, 111–13; LVIII, 27–8.

PAGE 119

1   *Ibid.* LIV, 314–19; LVI, 1–5.

PAGE 120

1   *Cambridge Retrospect,* 110; H. G. Wood, *Terrot Reaveley Glover,* 142–3.

PAGE 121

1   Council Minute, 1263/5.
2   *Ibid.* 1041/8, 1055/7, 1071/4, 1088/6, 1125/5.
3   *Ibid.* 1063/26.

PAGE 123

1   *Ibid.* 1237/6.
2   *Ibid.* 1473/10.

PAGE 124

1   *Ibid.* 1048/8.

PAGE 125

1   The point is made by Benians even for the eighteenth century: *Eagle*, LIV, 76.
2   The figures are from a report to the tutors and the college council by C. K. and G. C. L. Bertram.

PAGE 126

1   The phrase, of course, is Newman's, quoted Benians, *Eagle*, LIII, 3.

PAGE 127

1   *Ibid.* LV, 6.

PAGE 128

1   See generally, his lecture on *John Fisher* published by the Cambridge University Press in 1935 and *Eagle*, LI, 97 *sqq.*; LIII, 1 *sqq.*

INDEX

INDEX

Ogden, Samuel, 54, 58–9, 63, 65–6, 68, 82
Orchard, Arthur, 56
Osler, William, 105
Ospringe (Kent), 5–6

Page, Thomas Ethelbert, 87
Palmer, Edward Henry, 86, 103
Palmer, John Henry, 124
Paranjpye, Raghunath Purushottan, 100
Parkinson, Stephen, 79
Parsons, Sir Charles Algernon, 93
Pearce, William, 57
Pegge, Samuel, 63
Pember, Robert, 12
Pendlebury, Richard, 88
Penrose, Francis Cranmer, 92
pensioners, 10, 30–1
Percy, Alan (master), 8
Pevsner, Nicolaus, 76, 129
Pieters, John William, 88, 96
Pilkington, Leonard (master), 18–19
Pilkington, James (master), 18
Platt, William, 48
Pooley, Henry Fletcher, 93
Powell, William Samuel (master), 50, 57, 64 sqq., 89, 120
Previté-Orton, Charles William, 106
Prior, Matthew, 53
Pryme, Abraham de la, 44, 61, 63

Radnor, William Pleydell-Bouverie, earl of, 74–5
Raikes, Richard, 57
Rapson, Edward James, 102–3, 110
Reculver, Richard, 6
Redman, John, 12
religious tests, 67, 74, 89
research students, 100–1, 116–18
Reyner, George Fearns, 89
Rickman, Thomas, 76
Rivers, William Halse Rivers, 106
Robinson, Matthew, 37, 39–40
Roby, Henry John, 78–9, 84–5, 93
Rokeby, Sir Richard, 5
Rolleston, Sir Humphry Davy, 93, 122
Roper, Francis, 56
Ross, John (bishop of Exeter), 54
Russell Smith, Hugh Francis, 109, 112
Rutherford, Thomas, 56, 65
Rutland, John Manners, earl of, 47

St John's College, Cambridge
ball, 109
bursars, 9, 50, 57, 69, 82–3, 96–7, 107, 122–3
choir, 22, 43, 66, 73–4, 81–2, 108, 124–5
choir school, 73–4, 108, 124
council, 90, 110–11
deans, 7–9, 49, 63
endowments and revenues, 4–6, 27–9, 48–51, 67, 76, 82–6, 90–2, 96–7, 110, 121–3
examinations, 66–9, 86, 110
grounds, 7, 27, 48, 67, 76–7, 94, 119
laboratories, 85–6, 92, 103
lecturers, lectures, 12–13, 38–9, 55–7, 78–9, 84–8, 91–2, 103–6, 110–11
livings, 51–2, 82, 107
master, 1, 7–9, 18, 20, 28, 49–50, 63, 90
observatory, 66
organ, organist, 22, 43, 73–4, 91, 94, 124
plate, 22
plays, 36–7
president, 8–9
prizes, 47, 66, 74–5, 99
rooms, 7–8, 25–7, 47–8, 67, 73, 76, 93, 118–19
servants, 9, 11, 123–4
societies, 94, 108–9
sports, 13–14, 27, 36, 81, 94, 108–9, 125–6
steward, 9, 49
supervision, supervisors, 103–6, 120–1
tutors, 38–41, 52, 56–7, 63, 78–9, 84–6, 94, 107, 123
see also buildings, coaching, degrees, Eagle, exhibitioners, fellow commoners, fellows, Linacre lecturer, pensioners, religious tests, research students, scholars, sizars, statutes, studentships, undergraduates, visitor
St John the Evangelist, hospital of, 1–4, 6–7
Salisbury, William, 54–5
Scales, Oliver, 6
scholars, scholarships, 1, 5, 8 sqq., 26–7, 31–4, 63, 66, 80, 85–6, 98–100, 110, 116, 122
Ashton, 9
Bishop Fisher's, 5, 12, 18
Bishop Williams's, 26
Constable, 5
Dowman, 5, 9
foundress's, 8, 27
Lupton, 5, 9
Platt, 48
Thimbleby, 9

148

schools
  Aldenham, 32–3
  Bury St Edmunds, 33
  Durham, 48
  Eton, 59
  Hawkshead, 69
  Heath Grammar, Halifax, 58
  Hereford, 48
  Manchester Grammar, 48
  Marlborough, 82
  Marlborough Grammar, 48
  Oakham, 33
  Oundle, 33
  Peterborough, 33
  Pocklington, 5, 32
  Rivington and Black Rod, 32
  Rugby, 82
  Sedbergh, 5, 32, 59
  Shrewsbury, 32, 73, 87
  Uppingham, 33
Scott, Christopher Charles, 124
Scott, Sir George Gilbert, 91
Scott, Sir Robert Forsyth (master), 95–7, 101, 114, 122, 129–30
Selwyn, George Augustus, 93
Selwyn, William, 91
Shepherd, Nicholas (master), 19
Shorton, Robert (master), 1, 6, 8
Shrewsbury, Mary, countess of, 25, 27, 34
Sikes, Edward Ernest, 105, 107
Simeon, Charles, 68
sizars, 5, 25, 30–1, 51, 60, 73–4, 80–1, 98
Smith, Robert, 63
Smith, Thomas, 75
Smoult, Thomas, 44
Sollas, William Johnson, 86
Somerset, Sarah Seymour, duchess of, 48
Stansfield (Suffolk), 58
statutes, college
  Bishop Fisher's, 4, 8 sqq., 34, 38–9
  Elizabeth I's, 11, 19–20, 29–30, 34, 37–8, 40, 75–6, 83–5
  Henry VIII's, 18, 29, 36, 38, 40
  1848, 83–4
  1857–60, 83, 85–6
  1882, 83, 90, 94–6, 102
  1926, 119–21
Stephen, Leslie, 70, 88
Still, John (master), 19
Strafford, Thomas Wentworth, earl of, 22, 32

Strathcona and Mount Royal, Donald Alexander Smith, Baron, 117
studentships, 101, 117, 121–2
  Ann Fry, 101
  Baylis, 117, 143
  Hutchinson, 101, 117
  McMahon law, 93
  Naden, 101, 117
  Rolleston, 122
  Slater, 101, 117
  Strathcona, 117
Sylvester, John Joseph, 74, 78
Symons, Ralph, 25

Tanner, Joseph Robson, 98, 103, 106–7
Tarporley (Cheshire), 54
Tatham, Ralph (master), 77
Taylor, Charles (master), 95–6, 101, 109, 111–12
Taylor, John (master), 17
Taylor, John (senior bursar), 50, 52
Taylor, John ('Demosthenes'), 55, 57–8
Teall, Jethro, 86
Tennyson, George, 69
Thimbleby, Thomas, 5, 9
Thoday, Ralph E., 124
Thomson, Sir Joseph John, 100, 106
Todhunter, Isaac, 87–8
Tooke, John Horne, 70
Tuckney, Anthony (master), 23–4, 42–3
Turner, Francis (master), 43–4, 47

Ufford-cum-Bainton (Northamptonshire), 52
undergraduates, 7, 10 sqq., 30 sqq., 34 sqq., 59 sqq., 71–2, 80–1, 87, 92–4, 98 sqq., 107–9, 115 sqq., 125–6
  backgrounds of, 30–3, 35–6, 59–60, 71–2, 80, 92
  numbers of, 8, 24, 47, 59–60, 67, 71–2, 93, 98, 109–10, 114–15
  studies of, 11 sqq., 37 sqq., 61 sqq., 71, 77, 86–7, 98–9, 115–16, 121
Union Society, 73, 100

Vergil, Polydore, 3
Villiers, John Charles, 75
visitor, bishop of Ely as, 3, 18–20, 28, 75, 83–4

Wace, Henry, 87
Waideson, Robert, 22

INDEX